Praise for
Conversations with Thoth
and Pat Heydlauff

"*Conversations with Thoth* is a powerful book that reveals the secrets of the universe for manifestation and transformation. Pat Heydlauff is a pioneer in her field who lights the way for a better tomorrow. She has a special gift to hear spirits of light from beyond and is guided to write their messages and deliver them to humankind. *Conversations with Thoth*, which provides keys for spiritual enlightenment and personal growth, is a riveting, must-read for all!"

–Monet Brooks
Clairvoyant, Medium, and Spiritual teacher

"After reading *Looking Within* [the book Thoth refers to often] written by Pat Heydlauff, I purchased numerous copies to give as a gift to each of our employees. No matter one's situation or current difficulties, or just for self-improvement, this book aids the reader to reconnect with oneself in order to find a path of peace, calmness, and understanding of self. It's recognized that you can't depend on others for happiness but rather find happiness from within. Pat consistently focuses on the core 7 principles of aiding the reader to become or stay aligned in finding one's inner peace. Her message will help people embrace oneself to truly accept oneself. Thank you, Pat Heydlauff, for writing this book. Well done!"

–Janet MacLean Jansen
Owner of Windkiss Ranch and Co-Founder/Owner
of GypsyLive

"Whether you're seeking guidance in navigating life's challenges, exploring the mysteries of the universe, or simply yearning for a deeper connection to your inner self, Pat Heydlauff's books are a sanctuary for the seeker. Dive into the pages and let her words awaken your spirit, helping you find serenity, wisdom, and spiritual fulfillment."

—Kimberly Netling, DAOM, Vim Acupuncture and Integrated Wellness Center

CONVERSATIONS WITH THOTH

YOUR PATHWAY TO WISDOM, TRUTH, AND UNCONDITIONAL LOVE

Pat Heydlauff

Conversations with Thoth: Your Pathway to Wisdom, Truth, and Unconditional Love
Copyright © 2024 by Pat Heydlauff

All rights reserved. No part of this book may be used or reproduced by any means, graphic, electronic, or mechanical, including photocopying, recording, taping, or by any information system without the written permission of the publisher, except in the case of brief quotations embodied in critical articles and reviews.

ISBN: 978-0-9983347-9-0
Published by: Energy Design

Other Books by Pat Heydlauff
Looking Within: Discover 7 Principles Leading to Hope, Peace, and Joy
Feng Shui So Easy a Child Can Do It
Selling Your Home with a Competitive Edge
21 Ways…to Increase Employee Engagement
The Way We Go: Your Roadmap to a Better Future

To those who believe that wisdom, truth, and unconditional love are the way to the future we seek, and that a better, more peace-filled world lies ahead.

Acknowledgements

First and foremost, if I didn't have my deep and abiding connection to my Creator, God, First Source, the Divine, none of my books would have become a reality. It is through this Divine guidance that all my creativity flows, all my information comes to me, and I am sent various spiritual guides to give me direction and encouragement on my lifelong journey. I am filled with honor and gratitude for my Creator's omnipresence. I cannot recall a day that I did not know God was with me.

I'd like to thank Thoth for boldly entering my world and sharing his wisdom, knowledge, and unconditional love on such an experiential level. Without Thoth, no conversations could have taken place, no teaching done, and no experiential wisdom given. I honor and respect him for all he has given us through this collaboration and in millennia past.

Additionally, I'd like to thank my granddaughter, Erica West, for bringing to life some of the visual depictions of my experiences, both on the cover of the book and the sketches within the book. The book cover depicts the library corridor as I saw it when I first entered the Library of Wisdom and Knowledge. I'd also like to thank my team who made the publication of this book possible. To my editor, Dawn Josephson, a word and grammar magician who can take my ramblings or my conversations in this case and turn them into a masterpiece. And to Janet Aiossa, my graphic artist par excellence who has created the exceptional covers for each of my books.

There are a few others who I need to mention here—friends and colleagues who keep my spirits up, encourage me, keep me energized, and just help me cross over the finish line. They are Susan Wallace, my astrology guru, Rev. Monet Brooks, my intuitive consultant, Kim Netling, my wellbeing coach and NAET specialist, and Debbie Martens, a spiritually connected PLR guide.

And finally, I want to thank YOU, the reader. Without you, there would be no writers, no scribes, no need for books whether in print or digital. It is you, the reader, who every author wishes to connect with. In my case, I not only wish to connect with you but also to touch your heart so you can create a better future—a wonderful new future you deserve filled with wisdom, truth, and unconditional love.

Introduction

At the ripe old age of 10, I received a marvelous gift—one of those large Golden Books. I don't recall the book's actual title, but it featured all the countries of the world. Eager to devour this book, I flipped it open to a random page and saw a magnificent picture of the Great Pyramid, the Giza plateau, and information about Ancient Egypt as a two-page spread. I had never seen a pyramid before and found its unique shape with its many interior tunnels both intriguing and mesmerizing. I was in love. I stared at that magnificent piece of architecture and its internal passages for a very long time.

Then my eyes drifted to the bottom of the page, which featured many gods and goddesses recognized as the leadership of this strange and captivating land. For some reason, my attention was drawn to the image of the man with the ibis bird's head. I had never seen that type of bird before, as they were not native to where I grew up.

The years passed and I progressed through the educational system where I would occasionally see and study that same pyramid and the leaders of that land—leaders with the strange heads. More years passed and I continued to be drawn to the memory of that picture, which was now embedded into my mind. When documentaries about Egypt aired, I would be glued to the television watching them talk about the pyramids and unearthing the mummified pharaoh's bodies. I'm sure my children would have preferred viewing a cartoon or an age-appropriate sitcom.

In the late 1970s, I had the good fortune of being in New York when the Metropolitan Museum was featuring the traveling Egyptian exhibition, "Treasures of Tutankhamun." Nothing could keep me from attending the exhibit. I slowly experienced each display and took in all the history and magnificence of this exotic land.

Several years later, I started my spiritual journey. Even though I was going into the unknown, it still seemed much less fearful than avoiding it. I needed to learn everything I could, so I plunged ahead without reservation. At first, I experienced a lot of frustration due to my lack of understanding and clarity, but I pushed through with no reservations. At one point, a book called *The Emerald Tablets of Thoth the Atlantean* fell into my hands. Once again, I was drawn to Thoth, the Egyptian god with the bird head. By then I knew that the bird was an ibis and saw them regularly once I moved to Florida. The ibis is symbolic of balance, adaptability, purity, mystery, and unity, and their white color implies a sense of purity with powerful magic in their silence. I wondered at the time if Thoth also represented the same characteristics in ancient times.

I can't tell you how many times I've re-read that first book. Many additional books about Thoth and Egypt have appeared to me over the years, a few of which I've added to my collection. Additionally, I would occasionally see an ibis bird or two in my backyard, but I never paid them much attention. One day I took my little dog for a walk and noticed an ibis feather sticking straight into the ground, almost as if someone threw it like a dart and spiked it. I thought it was strange and wondered if I should pick it up. I didn't and continued my walk home. The next day I repeated the same walk, and that same feather was still waiting for me. That's when I realized it was a message. I picked up the feather and took it home, giving it a space of honor on my writing table.

As I continued my spiritual journey within, I have written several books, one building upon the other. But I still felt a sense of something missing. Not only do I journal almost daily, but I also journal manifestation requests or longings. On January 13, 2021, I wrote the following manifestation message to God, my Creator: "What would be the benefit to You, the universe, humanity, and me of having a one-on-one conversation with Thoth?" I was truly seeking ancient wisdom and knowledge that would benefit humanity in our 21st century lifestyle. Thoth has always been well known for being the god of wisdom and knowledge, magic, mathematics, the 365-day calendar, medicine, and science among several other things. This made Thoth the perfect guide.

During that same time period I was quite busy finishing the first draft of my most recent book, *Looking Within: Discover 7 Principles Leading to Hope, Peace, and Joy*, plus relocating my home. As I was settling in to my new home my journaling took a back seat for almost a year, but once you start journaling, you can never really stop. It will be only a matter of time before you return to it. I feel so connected spiritually when journaling that I long for it when I stop doing it for any length of time. That longing started to overshadow my life as I returned to writing, publishing my book, and spiritual teaching.

I felt the need once again for attaining a deeper level of meaning and information in the area of wisdom and knowledge, so on March 3, 2023, I wrote in my journal a second time about manifesting "easy access to wisdom and knowledge and the ability to recall it effortlessly so it could touch human hearts." This is where the story begins.

May the words in this book touch you in your heart center, nurture and nourish you, and provide you a new empowering lifestyle filled with unconditional love, peace, and joy.

Conversations with Thoth

"We begin! Close your eyes so you can hear. Listen carefully. It is I, Thoth, your trusted associate. We have both traveled many lifetimes and in many worlds since we last met and spent time in each other's presence. At that time, our relationship was teacher/student. I learned much from you because you were from the human side and I was an implanted Atlantean, a spirit, a god manifested in a human form and wearing an ibis headdress.

"You learned all I taught and spoke. You retained all that information within. We created a seal so only you and I together could release that ancient wisdom and knowledge. Humanity is ready to receive all that you have within. The time is now to break that seal.

"Mentally, lie flat on your back on a smooth surface like a bed or floor. I now stand by your left side with hands outstretched over your upper body, from your throat to your waist. Feel the deeply penetrating energy drop into that whole area of your body. It will feel like the summer sun burning a hole into the upper center of your body. Continue to lie in peace and comfort. Let the sun pierce through any protective shields you have surrounding you, as this is a benevolent sun beam with laser focus. Allow it to completely penetrate your body. It will pierce the center point of your chest cavity right beside your heart in alignment with your spine.

"At that point is located a mini treasure trunk that is locked with an ancient seal we both attached before placing it within you. We merged our marker on that seal, signifying that only the two of us have the right to break the seal and open the box at some time in the future when we would meet again. That time is now, today. As the box is located adjacent to your heart on the spine, you need to remain very still, quiet, and at peace for the sun to penetrate and break the seal.

"Success! It is officially unsealed today at 12:03 pm EDT. The information within is now accessible, but only to you. No one else is allowed access within.

"To access the information now that the seal is gone, you will simply unlock the treasure box door by your thought and a touch to the left side of your chest using your left hand and left ring finger. To close it you will simply reverse the process with a thought and a touch.

"Everything in there is organized by subject and is cross referenced many ways. It was these files you saw in your heart center the first time you ran an energy clearing meditation. You knew there was something beneath you in your meditation room within and believed it to be a vast library. Only you could see it. Now you know and understand what you saw—the contents of the wisdom and knowledge library within.

"Yes, you will need to remain diligent about opening and reclosing the chest so no one else can enter. You will not need to actually open the chest and wander through the millennia of information. Your thought will simply bring it to you, whether you are in silence or in a crowded room. You will also start to see things appear that you need to take notice of and instantly receive and understand the message.

"Ancient wisdom and knowledge have arrived."

Besides being in shock, I was also honored and grateful. More than two years had passed since I last mentioned Thoth's name in my journaling.

Thoth continued about how to physically enter the Library of Wisdom and Knowledge. "It is the same way we entered together thousands of years ago." By now it was nighttime and we were instantly transported to the physical entrance of the Library of Wisdom and Knowledge, somewhere in the infinite miles of sand and desert in Egypt. As we stood in front of an enormous wall of stone, Thoth unlocked a massive library door with his thought. The door appeared out of nowhere.

Upon entering this underground cavern that reached as far as the eye could see, Thoth said, "Go to the center of the cross point; stand in the middle of the symbol on the floor that contains the energy of only those who are allowed entry." A light appeared ahead of me as he spoke, showing me where to go. "Stand there solidly in place with bare feet planted on that symbol. It will have a definite geometric shape and look a little like a hexagon and a circle. The circle represents all wisdom and knowledge, completion, perfection, and God; the hexagon represents equilibrium or yin and yang, the unity of two poles of nature, north/south, above/below, spirit/matter, masculine/feminine, heaven/earth.

"Once the symbol recognizes you, by thought you can extract or recall any information you require or request. You can receive answers you seek to questions known or unknown. You have no limitations to this wisdom and knowledge other than time. This Library will provide you any information you seek or that it deems society could, should, or needs to understand at that moment in time, as well as wisdom and knowledge you need for self-growth.

"Your only rules are to be alone in a private, silent space. Connect with your heart center and unlock the massive doors to enter, then make your way to the center floor symbol. If you are deemed safe and private, all information will be available to you. There is only one caution, you need to be sure you have a clear vision of what you want to know and whether you want to see the circumstances surrounding that information."

I responded to all Thoth told me. "My precious Thoth, thank you for coming forward to help me after so many millennia have passed. I honor and recognize your greatness and am humbled by your commitment to help me. Please help me be wise and manifest all that I can share in this lifetime to serve others and create heaven on Earth."

Thoth spoke, "You honor me by seeking out all the wisdom you so carefully observed, wrote, and remembered from the past. Not only did you quietly keep the messages, wisdom, and knowledge hidden and guarded its preciousness with your life for all these years, but also you sought me out. We are now one, a team of two uniting to rebirth a Golden Age of society, a Renaissance of Joy on planet Earth.

"It begins now, today, this moment. The blessings of the ancients reside within you forever today and moving forward."

A New Day

"Your journey continues," Thoth said as he and I walked down a very long, low-lit corridor built before Ancient Egypt began. "When you were in the Library last, you finished your knowledge of how to use the Library. You can access its ancient mysteries at a moment's notice and speak about it in your current day language. We are now headed to my personal Abode."

Yes, in case you are wondering, Thoth lives below the surface of the Earth when not performing his duties as a god of high rank in the Ancient Egyptian hierarchy and today as Emissary of our Creator and the Sovereign Leader of the universe. His personal surroundings are in one massive chamber on the right side of the corridor that continued onward as far as I could see. We stopped walking and giant double doors reaching eleven feet upward appeared out of the library walls and slid towards us. The depth of the doors was the depth of the library shelves plus the granite walls. They parted in the middle and slid to the right and left as if on cue.

The doors made no sound as we proceeded through the opening, which closed within seconds after us. It was almost as it these doors were moved by an invisible force. Thoth gave me a reassuring glance as we stepped into a cavernous chamber filled with more books, technical devices, and computer-like instruments at one end and something more like a living room and dining area at the other end.

The chamber was well lit, almost as if daylight had somehow entered this space, which was impossible because it was nighttime outside and we were at quite a depth underground based on our long walk. Just as magically as the doors had opened and closed, food and drink appeared on a table on the opposite side of the room. The table had two chairs placed on an angle on opposite sides.

Thoth spoke of many things he had experienced and done in his lifetimes as we ate and drank. I saw no one else while eating, although I thought I felt the presence of some assistants nearby. For the most part, it seemed like things happened or were created by thought. Thoth beckoned me to follow him into another room he called the Sleep Chamber so I could rest. He told me to stay there and then he went further down the hall into another chamber where he would sleep and regenerate. He took one last look at me to make sure I was okay before disappearing.

I did not feel any fear. I wondered about the surroundings we were in and what we were doing there. I marveled a bit about the simplicity yet opulence of our surroundings underground and how it was all somehow connected to the ancient Library of Wisdom and Knowledge.

I didn't wonder long, as I greatly needed sleep and regeneration as well. Again, as if on cue, the lights dimmed very low, this time coming from along the floor. I still saw everything but there was no fear, no concern, no claustrophobia—all things I would experience above ground as a human under such circumstances.

Time passed quickly. As before, the full daytime lights slowly came on, letting my body know another day had arrived. Quite suddenly, Thoth and I were sitting together on opposite sides of the table discussing everything from technology and the items at the other end of the room to the esoteric.

At this point, Thoth pointed to a symbol on the floor in the center of the other half of the room. He explained, "You use that symbol the same way as the one in the main Library cross. Go. Stand on the symbol so it will recognize your energy field. From that moment onward, you can access this highly guarded technological information and esoteric wisdom at a moment's notice. But be warned. This information should be shared only when and if no other solution is available."

Once I completed the task, food and drink appeared again for nourishment and pleasure. It was beautiful, wonderful, sumptuous, and awe inspiring all at the same time.

Thoth spoke, "This is your sanctuary now too, as it is mine. Come here often to regenerate and bathe in its energy."

His words continued to echo in my head as the main doors opened again. We left the magnificence of his Abode and ascended the long corridor we descended yesterday. I was no more than thinking of our long descent and how difficult it would be going up when, in an instant, we stood at the Library exit.

The Technology Chamber

It was nighttime and Thoth awaited my arrival at the Library's secret entrance. As I approached and exchanged silent greetings with him, the massive doors moved forward and slid sideways, immediately closing when we were safely within the entrance chamber. I sensed a bit of a smile and twinkle in Thoth's eyes as we proceeded in silence along the entrance chamber's dimly lit halls. With each step we passed thousands of documents, books, and rolled papyri.

We arrived at the symbol in the center of the cross and I couldn't help but examine it more closely. I noticed that the symbol had a dot in the center—something I didn't see last time. It clearly depicted yet another sacred geometric shape I recognized instantly as Thoth's own mark. The moment I recognized it, Thoth's eyes glistened, acknowledging my newfound revelation. Throughout history, Thoth was occasionally represented holding this symbol. When the Pleiadeans started communicating with me, they encouraged me to obtain and keep this symbol near me, as it would serve me well. In fact, I often kept that symbol in my hand when I journaled. Now I knew why.

Thoth continued down another very long, dimly lit corridor. We went a great distance but it also seemed like time sped up, suggesting we traveled the distance more rapidly.

We finally came to another set of massive doors that opened silently like the others, and closed swiftly behind us as we cleared the entrance. Once again, we were in another massive chamber that appeared to be the size of a football stadium, yet underground. How was this all created, I wondered. It was well lit with sunlight and cooled as if with an air conditioner, yet no equipment, noise, or power stations were anywhere to be seen or heard.

I had never seen any of these areas before when I last shared a lifetime with Thoth, only the Library itself. Even then, I would watch and observe Thoth, his use of wisdom and knowledge, but would never actually enter the Library's chambers. I never even knew that massive chambers existed at the ends of the various tunnels and corridors he guided me through. One could easily get lost in the maze of corridors, yet I felt no fear or anxiety of either getting out or not finding a way out. It seemed so peaceful; the silence was deafening but not frightening.

This new chamber we entered appeared to be something like a manufacturing or production facility. It was impeccably clean, well lit, smelled like an ocean breeze, and made my heart soar with possibilities. In fact, the mammoth chamber had a sky painted on the ceiling and the walls were painted like a pastoral landscape you'd see in the United States heartland with fields, tress, domestic animals, and crops. It did not reflect the landscape of Egypt in the 21st century.

I wondered what was the historical time reference for our meetings. Was it before the Sahara Desert took over Egypt and massive areas in Africa?

Thoth brought my attention back into the present with him in the chamber. Again, he acknowledged my inner thoughts and questions. As I looked around the chamber, I realized this space was some sort of technological laboratory. In one area rested massive crystals, some were huge and shaped like ancient Egyptian obelisks, while other very large pieces were laying on their sides. In another area were moving enlarged replicas of atoms, levers, catapults, and other strange machinery that hadn't been invented yet in the 21st century or had been lost to past advanced civilizations. In another area I saw miniscule models of the inner workings of things like computers and what we know today as smart phones. There were so many technological items and gold covered objects that I couldn't even guess as to what they were.

As we proceeded towards the center of the chamber, we came upon something I recognized immediately—a levitating clear crystal star tetrahedron, the size of a two story four-bedroom home. It was suspended in midair and was obviously working or operating. It rotated on an axis, so to speak, of one of its points, pointing down toward the Earth with the opposite point rising upward towards the universe. The axis was perfectly aligned with the axis of planet Earth yet there was nothing above it or below it holding it in place.

Thoth explained, "It is creating and running energy for everything in the Library and the entire underground complex, plus any nearby populated areas."

I stood there mesmerized. I could have watched it for hours, as it was quite hypnotic.

We had barely seen half of the Technology Chamber when food and drink magically appeared at another table with two chairs across the room. Thoth beckoned me to come, sit, eat, drink, and rest before we proceeded.

My Next Return

"You've been absent too long," said Thoth. "You have much to learn and much to see. I'm glad you are back. Let's go," said Thoth. He had a bit of a cheeky grin on his face, which remained somewhat hidden by his very recognizable ibis headdress.

We met again in the dark of night outside the massive invisible entrance to the Library of Wisdom and Knowledge. While not visible from the outside, the entrance reminded me of Hatshepsut's enormous temple of Deir el-Ba hari at current day Luxor in Egypt. The inside of the Library, however, did not look Egyptian or related to any particular time frame, era, or culture. No artwork adorned the corridor walls, as they were simply filled with knowledge, documents, papers, and information in many forms. Nothing else lined the long corridors. The ceilings were too high to get an idea of what they looked like. They seemed to fade away into darkness.

Thoth spoke again, "Remember to solidly plant your feet on the sacred symbol on the floor in the center of the corridor cross. The more often you enter this sacred space, the quicker you will complete the recognition of your energy field, which will allow you to pass through and even open the main door through the entrance process by your heart."

I asked him what would happen if someone else got through the door who wasn't supposed to be in here. Thoth explained, "It would be impossible to do so, but just in case, the contents of the shelves would be invisible to an intruder's eyes. If they happened to stand on the floor symbol, it would not only be non-responsive, but all corridors would disappear from sight. An energy force would physically remove the intruder from the Library and erase any memory the intruder may have left of the site, its location, and entrance."

By now, we had traveled what seemed like miles down the same corridor we went down during my last visit. Finally, we arrived in the same football stadium sized chamber with the massive pieces of crystal laying down and/or standing in the far corner, and a wide variety of tools, equipment, and micro-chip technologies I had never seen before and had no idea what their purpose or function was.

This time Thoth told me, "All you have to do is hover your hand over any piece of equipment or technology and it will immediately release all information to you in a download type action." He then warned me, "Do not touch the massive quartz crystals in the corner as they are still at maximum strength and could harm a human due to their high frequency. If you listen carefully, you will notice a low-pitched hum coming from them. They are currently being cleansed and will be prepared for human use in the form of energy. The tall obelisk was just completed and is ready to be moved where needed. If you hover your hand near it, it will reveal its location of origin, composition, and cleansing preparation process. Its basic framework is silicon-oxygen tetrahedra with each oxygen being shared with two tetrahedra."

I couldn't help but note the two tetrahedra in its composition as I turned back to look at the huge star tetrahedron continually rotating. A quiet smile of acknowledgement radiated on Thoth's face.

Finally, we arrived again at the massive star tetrahedron, which continued its endless journey of generating energy. As we neared it, I faintly heard a low-pitched, semi-silent hum coming from it. I suspected I was being allowed to hear it; for others it would likely be complete silence.

Food appeared across the room. We sat, ate, drank, and refreshed ourselves before moving on.

"Now let's turn our attention to the other end of the chamber," Thoth said as he nodded his head in the opposite direction from the crystals and mechanical and technical equipment. I looked in the direction he indicated. Coming into clear view were what seemed like lush farm land, crops, trees, and animals, both domesticated and wild. There appeared to be an invisible separation between the animals. The wild animals such as lions, tigers, and elephants did not mingle with the cows, oxen, camels, horses, dogs, and cats. The entire area seemed to be filled with peace and love. There was no anguish, no fear, and no dominion over others. While no humans were present, I sensed they were there, just not visible to me. Thoth nodded his head in agreement and spoke, "This is heaven on Earth. It is the way Earth was designed before greed, power, and enslavement by the powerful became the norm." He equated my book, *Looking Within*, to what I was seeing. "Once again, that eternal dream and original design of the Creator has been put forth for humanity to see and experience through your book. It is important for you to see this in reality. The people in those homes and cities hide from you in case you are an overlord and wish to control and enslave them again."

I knew I was in a building but it seemed like I was viewing hundreds of acres of land, cities, and villages. Right next door, the wild beasts of prey laid peacefully next to each other, basking in the warmth of the sunlight as if they were at peace with each other and the world.

Responding to my unspoken thoughts, Thoth said, "No more cages, no more poaching, no more circus acts with malicious whips snapping. This is also their heaven on Earth as it is described in your book."

While the light remained, the view began to dim and fade out of sight as if it were all a movie production for my eyes only. Thoth beckoned me by saying, "We have much work to do. In the human world your work has just begun. We will travel this journey together and share our Creator connection for the good of humanity, the universe, and our Creator, the One."

The Healing Chamber

"Come, this way." Thoth welcomed me and encouraged me to hurry to the invisible wall opening to the Library of Wisdom and Knowledge. This time he motioned for me to precede him well before we reached the location of the door.

As if on cue, the door quickly recognized my spiritual essence. Without a sound, the door appeared and slid aside for us to enter. Like always, we barely crossed the threshold and the door quickly and silently closed, securing us and our privacy within. As usual, the lights were dim but accurately reflected the corridors into an otherwise dark abyss. He sent me on ahead to the floor symbol to activate the energy field ahead. As I neared the symbol on the floor, the symbol recognized my energy field and a light appeared on the corridor straight ahead, giving me passage information as to which direction to go.

We walked side-by-side in silence yet still had a wonderful interaction and exchange of information on an energy level. I found the process amazing and awe inspiring. I wished I could have such interactions in my daily human life. At that very instant Thoth stopped, looked directly into my eyes, and said out loud, "What is preventing you from doing that right now?"

I must have looked shocked, as he spoke again. "Communicating through thought using brain waves is quite possible on Earth. Have you tried? All you need are two people on the same spiritual wave length and thought communication is quite possible. Use your brain waves like telepathy to send your thoughts to the intended person. If you are close to the same level of spiritual awareness, the other person will receive and respond.

"You and I have been doing this ever since we've rejoined our energetic fields and wave lengths. We were unable to do this when you were in my lifetime as a young male scribe, but you have tremendously grown through many lifetimes and are at a spiritual energetic level that allows us to communicate through our energy field brain waves. In fact, we have exchanged very few verbal words; almost all communication has been through intended internal brain wave exchange."

I immediately thought of a few people I might like to experiment with using this form of communication in my human life. Not only is it silent but also very private.

Thoth winked as if acknowledging my complete understanding of his instruction.

We walked quite a distance and nothing seemed to be in sight when suddenly a massive wall door appeared, much like the outside Library entrance, and opened, allowing us just enough time to step through before it immediately slid shut behind us, again in complete silence.

However, this time we were in a small sort of holding room. It felt like we were in a purification chamber, perhaps a holding cell that ensured our physical and spiritual purity. Thoth nodded his head in agreement, confirming that I understood what was happening.

After what seemed like several minutes but probably was only a few seconds, a second wall door opened in front of us into another huge chamber, albeit not as large as the Technology Chamber. This chamber was varying shades of pastel blue, pastel green, and cotton candy pink.

The walls were painted in the three colors in a slight wave pattern with splashes (elongated 3-inch-wide slices) of pink merging in and out of the soft blue and green shades. The walls appeared to almost move with the energy the colors created. I noticed more green than blue. The wave colors were painted approximately six inches wide and swept in and out of each other. Even the brush strokes were evident. The ceiling was painted a darker blue with a full astronomical map of the stars visible to humans in the early evening sky.

Thoth explained, "This is our Healing Chamber." I looked around. The chamber was filled with unusual beds that looked more like transparent floating space capsules. Thoth acknowledged my observation and said, "Rather than a bed, we use healing chambers as well as other technology. Many of these things have not been discovered by humans yet or they are not recognized as healing and wellbeing methods in your culture. Notice the capsules. You can easily see in and out of the beds, which is good for the patient, their family, and the care giving team. The transparent carts beside each bed hold crystals of varying sizes, shapes, and colors and are inserted into the beds at varying times of day for specific time lengths and in various colors to meet the healing needs of the patient. No drugs or allopathic medicines are used. We only use crystals, homeopathic remedies, colors as you can see on the walls, plants (I assumed he meant herbs), and meals formulated for each patient's maximum healing potential.

"Some beds have canopies that slide over the top to protect privacy and promote healing, as if in meditation, or rest without distractions. Everything is computer generated except for the touch aspect. Care givers and loved ones can and do appear at a moment's notice to aid in the healing process. The patient is never alone for any length of time because the energetic love of another human is essential to the healing process.

"We do no invasive allopathic methods here, only healing. The prime source for healing comes from sound, energy frequencies, colors, and the vibration of the crystals. The crystals used for this process, unlike those in the Technology Chamber area, are all quarantined, purified, and finely tuned to healing frequencies to meet the various needs of each patient. Once a crystal is no longer needed by that patient, it will be returned to quarantine, cleansed, recalibrated, and reused.

"When patients are done in their bed for the day, they will move to the spa for soaking in special mineral waters, a massage, or other treatments like Reiki, yoga, or Tai Chi type activities. Once done there they go to the social area or the dining room and enjoy food, drink, and the company of family and friends."

Thoth motioned for me to follow. We walked quite a distance past many beds. Once again, we sat, ate, drank, and rested. I noticed that every time we sat at the table our chairs were on opposite sides of the table at a 45-degree angle to the table. We never sat directly facing each other. Our extended conversations over food always took place at a bit of a distance, at least a seated angular distance.

As we finished our rest, he mentioned that he had a brief side trip for me before we returned to the real world. We walked toward a wall opposite the chamber entrance. Much to my surprise, another door opened and we entered another small purification room. We stood there for a moment before another set of doors opened.

The Healing Chamber we just left was quiet, serene, and had music or a pleasant sound. It felt much like the fragrance of flowers you couldn't see but knew they were there. The new chamber that appeared as the next set of doors opened in front of us was quite loud, in fact noisy. It was filled with all kinds of animals. Small ones like domestic cats and dogs were up off the floors with special sleeping mats at the bottom of their elevated sleeping areas. Others like cows, camels, oxen, and horses had much larger spaces, but all had specialized sleeping/healing mats using the same technology as on the human side. They were not exactly in cages but each animal seemed to know its boundaries and remained in the specific spaces created just for them.

As you might expect, since this chamber was filled with animals, the space was massive and handled both large and small animals. Thoth spoke, "There is also a section for serious wildlife such as tigers, lions, bulls, camels, and elephants. There is even a section for birds like cranes and ibis. When they are done with their treatments, each is taken to their version of a play or exercise area, and for feeding and sleeping where they will stay until their next time on their healing mats."

This was such a wonderful room. I could have spent hours there talking to and petting the animals. Thoth observed and smiled.

The next thing I was aware of, we were back where we began, on the outside of the massive Library doors that were now well hidden in the wall of rock. Thoth bid me a reassuring farewell for the day.

The Creativity Chamber

"Hurry. I have something I must show you NOW!" Thoth motioned for me to come quickly, which was humorous as I was standing only 12 inches from him when we both arrived at our usual meeting place in the darkness. The only obvious light in the sky came from the stars twinkling brightly above. In fact, they seemed particularly bright on this night.

Thoth realized my focus was on the stars so he tugged on my clothing to get my attention. Off we went in the blink of an eye. Not only had we entered the Library and passed over the symbol, but were down one of the long corridors again. Finally, we stopped. We turned to the left. A whole section of Library shelves moved forward and parted like the doors to the various other chambers we entered, or for that matter, the Library itself.

I could tell Thoth was very excited for me to enter this chamber. He almost looked gleeful and childlike as the doors opened. This chamber overflowed with laughter, joy, and music, yet somehow was creative and peaceful. I'm not sure how else to describe what I was feeling and experiencing. It almost felt like joy-filled organized chaos.

The chamber was filled with lots of light but no direct sunlight. Even though I had visited Thoth's underground fortress several times, I still marveled at the light considering everything was chiseled out of stone and in some cases hundreds of feet below ground. This room made my heart soar like on the wings of an eagle or perhaps in this case, an ibis. The highs and lows and everything in between were magnificent at its least and resplendent with joy, love, and exhilaration at it best.

Thoth explained, "We are in the Creativity Chamber, the creative center of our solar system. In one area there are musicians, where you can see Mozart composing one of his famous pieces like The Marriage of Figaro, right next to indigenous people creating their version of singing and dancing to the beat of sticks, drums, and rattles. Others are playing harpsicords, cimbaloms, and the balalaika. Just a little further down is Johann Strauss II composing waltzes like the Blue Danube. You can also see contemporary era conductor Arthur Fiedler, who excelled at adapting popular and classical music for orchestra performance, and composer John Williams with hits like the themes for Star Wars, ET, and Harry Potter.

"There are hundreds of musicians, singers, and dancers from ancient lifetimes to the more current genres like rock, country, Latino, Native American, and ballad. Even present are Elvis and the Beatles. No matter where you look, you can experience music, whether it is from children's choirs, ancient Roman organs, or Predynastic Old Kingdom Egyptians using harps, flutes, lyres, and percussion."

One by one, scenes came to life as my eyes focused on each vignette. Thoth also came to life knowing how much I would enjoy this area. I likened it to a 1960's Woodstock experience on steroids. Thoth encouraged me to move on. "There is more to come," he said. In fact, there was so much to see that as a human I could barely take it in much less process it.

As we traveled through the Creativity Chamber, we moved into the fine arts area, including painting and sculpting. First came some of the cave dwelling painters with their symbols and depictions of animals and primitive life. Thoth said, "Their creativity was symbolic of the fullest extent of their world knowledge at that time and the importance of the stars and solar system to their daily lives. The early artists from the Australian indigenous tribes, the Inca, the Mayan, and the Native Americans all depicted similar messages acknowledging the Earth, the directions, their living styles, and the heavens.

"As time passed you can see a very different form of art appear in Egypt with color, shape, and form, plus the addition of semi-precious stones and metals, especially gold. This area was very sophisticated and more accurate in depiction. By then, art was on walls, jewelry, and quite notably, architecture. Ancient Rome, Egypt, Greece, India, China, and the Middle East were all alive with sculptures, paintings, mosaics, and metal work. From the west coast of Europe to the far east of China and Japan, art was alive and well. Let us continue our journey. As you can see, we are traveling through many other eras."

Finally, we arrived in the Renaissance era with Michelangelo, Raphael, and Leonardo da Vinci, ending with Rembrandt. As I admired their work, it appeared as if da Vinci nodded to acknowledge me, and Rembrandt tipped his hat, as if they both recognized me. We continued our creativity journey through other artistic eras, finally reaching one of my favorites, the Impressionists. There they were: Monet in the garden by his house and Renoir nearby. Down just a little further were Mary Cassatt and Edger Degas, all working on canvasses, capturing the landscapes and models in everyday circumstances. We moved right on up to current times, but it was difficult to see, acknowledge, and write about. There were so many impressions and options. This chamber was indeed a library but instead of books and information it was about creativity at its best. I felt captivated and overwhelmed at the same time.

Next, we moved through the artform of dance, everything from participants at ancient religious events to the erotic to priests who danced with full armor carrying sacred shields. In Egypt they were skipping and leaping to hands clapping and percussion instruments. Thoth told me, "Dance showed up in 10,000 BC old rock shelter walls and 5,000-year-old tombs. It became much more of an art form as the years passed, moving into celebrations, theatrical dance, and ballet. It was a form of communication, celebration, healing, mourning, worship, and life.

"Aristotle spoke of dance as poetry with movement, expression, emotion, passion, and action. In India and China, dance dates back to the first millennium BC. It wasn't until the Renaissance that dance masters taught nobility the steps to what became ballet and dancing as a couple. Also following the Renaissance period, in the 17th century, the waltz began as a folk dance in Austria and Bavaria. That opened the doors to all forms of dance practiced in the 21st century."

Thoth could see that at this point I was beyond exhilarated and exhausted. He suggested we sit, partake of food and drink, and then rest.

Day Two at the Creativity Chamber

The next day I awakened, still underground in my sleep chamber just off the Great Room in Thoth's Abode. The lights came up slowly as if responding to my body. I heard Thoth's quiet voice within say, "Come, eat, drink, and prepare for another busy day of exploration." It was as if Thoth was a hologram encouraging me to rise and shine.

After some delicious nourishment, we returned to the Creativity Chamber and picked up where we left off. We moved from waltzes to free form dance that was reminiscent of the beauty and flow of movement of ancient religious worship and celebratory dance. As I watched, I realized that human dance was currently doing a reverse metamorphosis. In ancient times no one touched or looked at each other when they did touch. Between those generations and today, dancers fought for the right and joy to create together with eyes and bodies touching. Their eyes told as much of a story as did the movement of their bodies as they responded to the flow of the music. Now, in the present 21st century society, dance has reverted to safe space dancing with no direct contact or intimate connection.

We concluded the dance area with a sneak peak of ice skating, which at one time was only a way of travel, but then moved into entertainment, sports competition, and ice dancing. I could have stood there watching the gliding flow of the skaters forever, but I sensed the internal tug of Thoth to move on. He then said, "There are two more categories of creativity to experience."

Next came the authors, the writers, and the scribes. Everything was on display, from the ancient indigenous people's wall stories to Egyptian hieroglyphs to the individual stories of the Bible. Some of the scribes and authors were working on the Bhagavad Gita, others on Buddha's teachings called the Theravada, and yet others working on Taoism. Of course, there were many others from ancient times including those working on stone, clay, and papyrus.

Thoth explained, "Once Johannes Gutenberg invented the Gutenberg press in the mid-thirteenth century for book printing and reproduction, the race was on and books and the written word became the mode of the modern world for communication and entertainment. The doors of the written word were flung wide open for all levels of humanity to learn, experience, and feel wherever and whatever they wanted to experience. It also allowed for the massive expansion of servitude and control by others."

I saw everyone from Shakespeare to J. K. Rowling, from Greek and Roman philosophers to Jeffery Chaucer, and poets like Dante and Robert Frost. Front and center were cartoonists Bill Waterson of Calvin and Hobbs fame and Charles H. Schulz of Peanuts fame, including sketches of Charlie Brown and Snoopy, his infamous dog.

As we continued our journey, up next were the story tellers and cinematic script writers. Then came the movies and productions that brought stories to life on screen and stage. Again, the creative juices were flowing. Some black and white movies began late in the 19th century but really blossomed in the 20th century, bursting the magic glass ceiling of creativity.

The first motion picture house opened on Broadway in 1894. Soon followed film, all before the year 1900. The earliest films with international titles were *Scrooge* or *Marley's Ghost* in 1901, and a sci-fi movie called *A Trip to the Moon* in 1902. These movies paved the way for movies like *Sherlock Holmes Baffled* and *Alice in Wonderland* to the first true blockbusters, *Gone with the Wind, Citizen Kane, Singing in the Rain, Star Wars, It's a Wonderful Life, Raiders of the Lost Art, Harry Potter, Forrest Gump, Yankee Doodle Dandy,* and so many more.

As the cinematic industry grew, so did the audience and the size of the screen. Yet today, the size of the screen can be as small as the size of your computer or phone screen and viewed in a way that is totally disconnected from others.

As we left this magnificent room Thoth noted, "Everything you see in this chamber, even the artists and musicians, has gone through many cycles of being alone, an individual, to being connected and finding beauty, hope, joy, and peace, and now disconnected again, uncaring, searching, seeking, and unhappy. The Earth and the universe are made up of cycles. They are not obvious to most but the cycles are written in the stars and reflected in the seasons.

"This section of the Library is quite large. There is much emphasis placed on Creativity because it is the key to opening the human's heart to its connection with the Creator. The First Source, the One, God was and is the master of creation. Without creation there would only be void. The easiest way for humanity to find their way back to their Creator is through creativity. Each person should dedicate a portion of their lives every week to creative activities. There are so many to choose from. Exhibited here are only a few universally recognized creativities. Even bird watching is a creative activity.

"Additionally, creativity fills the heart with joy and reduces stress. It is an outlet that brings the human being back in control of their life and provides them peace within, allowing a spiritual flow of energy to freely move between the being and their Creator."

> "Creativity is the key to opening the human's heart to its connection with the Creator."

The Transportation Chamber

"We must go," said Thoth. "There is so much more to see and learn. It is time for you to experience the realities of tomorrow, the future, the wholesomeness of the new reality." Thoth spoke out loud this time. It surprised me yet gave me a sense of extreme importance as I rarely heard his voice. It was mid to upper range baritone in depth with resonance that caught me off guard. His voice was quite elegant and forceful yet somehow gentle and soft as freshly picked cotton. I didn't need to experience it directly to know that it could also be as ferocious as an angry lion or bellowing like a provoked bull. I am blessed and grateful to know him as a personal guide and companion.

I was so enamored by his voice that I didn't notice we were already down another corridor on our journey to wherever he was taking me. The Library walls opened and parted again, this time exposing another chamber filled with many strange and unusual items, perhaps machinery. This was obviously some type of engineering or mechanical room. I recognized little in the massive space.

He spoke out loud again, "This is the Transportation Chamber filled with what is to come. People will fly but not in oversized airplane cattle cars. They will sit in clear capsules in personal or group compartments and be whisked away as if riding on air waves (not to be confused with 21st century radio air waves). Travel will be silent with no pollution and provide almost door to door service. Some capsules will be much larger and provide amenities for long distance travel with few to no stops. Smaller ones will be used for local and commuter travel.

"Automobiles will be a thing of the past as will trucks and trains. Cargo will also be moved via capsule and will travel at lower heights to allow for their weight. All capsules, based on size and content, will travel at various heights for safety purposes much like airplanes do in the 21st century. Individuals and families may or may not have their own capsule for private use. Most will use public transportation due to ease of use and little or no cost.

"For those who wish to walk or take a stroll to a park, they will need no transportation vehicle. However, if their destination is at a distance, they can take their own hover platform or capsule for one or two people and ride at ground level. They will not drive but rather key in the destination location reference code; the capsule will automatically route itself based on the current physical conditions while the passenger sits back and enjoys the ride.

"For walking, exercise, and sporting activities there are parks, indoor/outdoor stadiums, arenas, and play areas where people can easily enjoy the outdoors. If the weather doesn't permit, some of the outdoor space can be temporarily enclosed so activities can continue uninhibited. While there will be many sporting activities, a much greater emphasis will be placed on the passive form of martial arts such as Tai Chi, Qigong, or contemporary versions of yoga. It's all about the movement and flow of energy in the body, not the power and strength of the human body. These forms will be taught at every level of schooling and every military, police, and firefighting academy. These methods are all about energy flow, strategy, and endurance, not brute force.

"Anything created for travel was done with perfect equilibrium, balance, and materials made for travel on the energy waves of the universe. The precision is the same as that of the Great Pyramid of Egypt and perfected beyond infinite measure."

Thoth noted my tiredness and low concentration and insisted we end the day early and begin anew tomorrow.

Day Two at the Transportation Chamber

The next day we were back in the Transportation Chamber. Thoth continued, "All vehicles or transportation carriers are transparent on the upper half so passengers have a full view of the outside surroundings. If the weather is inclement, the external view will be replaced with a pleasant internal reproduction of what should be outside at that time. If traveling in the dark, the full spectrum of the night sky or the universe will appear as the sun sets and changes before the sun rises again.

"Because of the waves you travel on, it is always smooth and never uncomfortable or long, even where global travel is involved. Crystals are not involved in the actual travel mechanism but the vehicles are connected to the Earth's energy created by polar magnetism." The closest reference I could relate this to was work done by Nicola Tesla.

Before moving along, and sensing that I was getting tired, I asked Thoth if he could help me prevent my instant and enormous drop in energy at the end of each day. He nodded with a twinkle in his eye as if to say, "What took you so long to ask." He answered out loud, "Soon."

As we continued walking, I noted that space travel was also very different than what we know in the 21st

century. Thoth spoke, "The space vehicles look much like the land vehicles. In fact, you can hardly tell them apart except for size. They are all bullet shaped except they come to a curved point on both ends for air flow and velocity. There are no propellant tanks on the bottom and no true landing pads. Universe travel is for both pleasure and scientific research. To depart you must go to a transportation hub, similar to current day airports. The capsule is loaded and then automatically moves onto a waiting transportation platform that routes it to its galactic vehicle. Personal belongings are placed in sealed travel bins before anyone enters the departure platform. There are no papers to show or ticketing inside. Everything is done through your personal energy identification code.

"Once aboard, people are shown to their seats. When all passengers have boarded, the vehicle leaves the transportation entrance platform and moves to the departure platform where it is merged with its power source. The vehicle is tilted slightly upward and slowly rises, as if the hand of the Creator is under it lifting it steadily upward, then thrusts it forward. Its speed is great and it moves out of sight instantly. There is no massive noise, no exhaust fumes, and no special clothing or helmets are required.

"Since the passengers might travel anywhere from a few hours to a few days, the vehicle has activity rooms, separate guest cubicles for work or silence, a place to eat, and their chairs become beds for sleep."

We continued our journey in what turned out to be a truly massive space. I noticed there were no ships, trains, and trucks on what were once highways, railways, and waterways—nothing that even resembled a garbage or fire truck. Thoth commented, "The air is pure and clean. Maintenance, repairs, and sanitation services are all underground. Everything creating pollution in the past is no longer needed and can be found in historical museums."

I marveled at the peace and quiet of all these transportation vehicles, almost in disbelief. Thoth smiled and said, "This is the future humanity will be creating once they have fully moved out of the Piscean energy age and proceeded well into the Aquarian age energy. This is the type of change to prepare for. These are the results of the vision you see in the future. You are helping to create it."

We rested again, ate, and drank before our journey for the day ended.

A New Day

"Focus," said Thoth. "We are here together. Sharing this time is like joining the energy of the moon and the sun. It's perfection."

It is always a joyous reunion with Thoth. I can never tell whether it's been minutes, hours, or days between visits. It always seems like only a milli-second passed between the time we spent thousands of years ago and today. There is a quiet, respectful joy when we are in each other's presence. When I am with him, I feel like it was just yesterday that I was a mere child following Thoth's every move and action so I could best serve him.

Although I still feel like I'm serving him, I also feel as if I've graduated from a student/teacher relationship to associate or colleague. It was an incredible honor yet very humbling. I always thought of him as a master teacher, the god of ancient wisdom and knowledge. Yet now, it appeared that he respected me and expected me to be a teacher too of ancient wisdom and knowledge.

Down the halls we traveled again, only this time we were back in the first room we visited when I arrived, the one with the highly secret, esoteric and information Library to the right and a personal seating area on the left with a private hall leading to the sleeping chambers on the far side of the room. We were back in Thoth's personal Abode.

As we sat and ate at the table across the room, Thoth reminded me, "From now on, this is your sanctuary too and you should feel free to explore and do what brings you joy." My mind raced with excitement as I tried to make sense of his words. In reality, nothing in this magnificent space was worthy of exploration versus spending time in Thoth's presence and energy field.

He obviously sensed my thoughts as his eyes twinkled, trying to hold back a creeping grin. Thoth was never depicted as someone with a personality and a sense of humor, but it became obvious that he was definitely quite personable. I never saw this side of him when he grabbed my arm as a young boy and quickly guided me into a space vehicle so many years ago as Atlantis sank. He hid me in the vehicle so the few others who escaped with him couldn't see me. While carefully disguising my location to keep me safe he whispered, "You are my student. You will help the world return to the Creator's origins in many millennia. It is important you remain safe and unknown to others. You will be my scribe and witness to all I say and do. When we are safely in our new land, I will come get you."

My next recollection was debarking from the vehicle in darkness of night and watching him quietly and ever so cautiously lower the vehicle down into the earth where it would remain safely sealed and cared for until needed again. That was the last time I ever saw his real face and the first time I saw him in his ibis headdress.

All these memories of everything we did together and I observed him doing in Ancient Egypt came flooding into my mind. I felt like I was like watching a slow-motion picture documentary in rewind mode. The emotions were strong, and my heart cried and ached for those wonderful memories of my past.

We sat in the chamber in silence for what seemed like hours, not saying one word out loud, but communicating and reflecting on the joy, heartaches, and happiness of our shared past. I didn't want this moment to end.

The Galaxy Chamber

That moment must have ended in sleep, as I awakened to daylight slowly revealing the beginning of another day.

Thoth spoke, "Wake up," beckoning me to come. I arose quickly and followed. His message was simple for our outing that day. "We always move forward using hindsight only for reference or gaining wisdom and knowledge. The future is created now, not tomorrow or yesterday. Tomorrow is created by the past and now creates the future."

As I continued to reflect on what he just said, he gave me quick side glance and said, "You'll have plenty of time to reflect later. Now is the time to move forward."

We didn't always take time for food; it seemed as if our bodies somehow regenerated and were nourished as we slept with no hunger upon awakening. We steadily moved down a side corridor, just outside and behind the same massive room referred to as home or the Abode. We stopped in front of another hidden massive door that opened as we approached and closed behind us, disappearing as quickly as it appeared. We stepped into another huge chamber that had a domed ceiling, the Galaxy Chamber. The chamber transformed from daylight to night based on the thought command given by the person in the room. It was like a planetarium for our galaxy where you could sit comfortably in gently swiveling chairs, view, and study any part of our solar system and the universe beyond. To make it easier for me, all the astrological or zodiac symbols took form and were sketched in so I could understand where we were in history at any given moment in time.

Thoth spoke for hours, "It's important for humans to understand the cycles of time and how they relate to where we are today—what the impact is of the twelve ages or houses of the zodiac as they cycle through every 26,000 years, taking approximately 2,000 years to move through each house.

"Humanity in the 21st century does not understand and respect the significant role each astrological house plays in the makeup of each society. In order to create a reign of hope, peace, and joy, humanity needs to learn about astrology and its impact on societal behaviors. When they understand that, the leaders of a society can create a foundation that will maintain hope, peace, and joy during a 2,000-year passage of a difficult astrological house and then learn to blossom and create an even better society in the next more friendly age.

"Society needs an astrological wakeup call. The 21st century will be full of massive change for the better. It will give birth to a spiritual awakening, a revival and rebirth of the arts, music, literature, and wonderful advances in the areas of health care, not disease care, and technology."

> "To create a reign of hope, peace, and joy, humanity needs to learn about astrology and its impact on society."

As the room reverted to daylight, I noticed what looked like a measuring tape at what seemed to be the equator level in the middle portion of the sphere. In some ways we appeared to be standing in the dead center of a sphere. If we looked up we saw the northern portion of the night sky, and if we looked down we saw the southern hemisphere night sky.

The same was true during the daylight hours, but I didn't understand the belt or band around the middle.

Thoth motioned and spoke, "Look closer." He explained, "The belt in the middle represents the span of the last 26,000 years. You will see there are time frames noted when civilizations began and ended. Dinosaurs lived and were destroyed. Massive flooding occurred, leading to death and destruction. You can see the time of Atlantis, the birth of Khem or Egypt, the Anunnaki, and ancient civilizations in India, China, and Cambodia. Upon examining each mentioned on the belt you will receive all the information you seek."

We spent much more time basking in the starlight absorbing its wisdom, and then finally returned to our sleep chambers.

An Unexpected Day

Another night passed and I was still underground in Thoth's Abode. As I awakened, I was somewhat unsettled that I did not hear Thoth's voice. I wondered if I had overslept or woke up early.

I went out into the grand hall or main room and saw food and drink, so I sat to enjoy my feast. Thoth was still not present, which took away a bit of the joy from the nourishment.

Just as I finished and started contemplating my next move, Thoth appeared in front of the entrance to the room. My heart skipped a beat as my ancient companion appeared. He promptly reminded me, "You are my associate, not just a companion."

He appeared to be in no hurry today. In fact, he seemed to relish the fact that we were experiencing the joy of peace and silence. After an extended period of quiet time, he spoke.

"It is at times like this that I experience pure joy and connection with all that is and can regenerate myself." He then drew in several very deep long breaths as if they were his last. It appeared as if he was in a deep trance far away. As he finished his last deep breath, he seemed to pop back into the present, welcoming me to the new day as he apologized for his late return. He said, "I'm famished," and ate his fill as we continued our conversation about the universe sphere we visited the day before.

I had so many questions. He responded, "You can visit any or all of these chambers and our home any time you wish and be given the answers you seek."

My heart wasn't sure how to react when he referenced this grand hall as ours. I wondered what he meant by that. Did he expect me to come here often? Alone? Without invitation? For reasons other than wisdom and knowledge such as rest and relaxation or to destress?

Forgetting that he could interpret the musings of my mind, he spoke. "Yes, to all the above. You are now as I. You can access information, regenerate, study, and absorb all. Your energy has fully integrated with the galactic systems and in turn it in you. Others will not know where you've gone or when you will return. You will be eternally safe wherever you travel, whatever you do, or whatever knowledge you seek. You will see truth that can be very painful at times. You will definitely see happiness and many forms of joy. In fact, they will be your favorite places to be.

"You can be here in the blink of the eye. Most of the time I will be here but you belong here whether I am here or absent. This is now our place of residence. You will always be graciously welcomed and want for nothing."

At this point he slowly raised both of his hands towards his head and even more slowly removed his ibis headdress, revealing distinct dark brown warm and welcoming eyes that could both pierce the soul or melt the heart. His high strong cheek bones looked a bit like that of a Native American, and his jaw line was somewhat square, giving his face perfect balance. He was neither young nor old with lots of dark soft wavy hair pulled back in something a bit like a flat pony tail. His eyes twinkled as he carefully studied my face while I watched in disbelief. After we left Atlantis and came to Egypt, I never saw his face again. He always wore his ibis headdress. That was his identity in Egypt for thousands of years, until this moment.

His ibis headdress, which he wore all the time, made him quite tall, but even without it, he was still tall and carved a statuesque figure. I had never seen him without the headdress in our previous lifetime after we left Atlantis or this one. I was stunned and didn't know how to react. At first, I was embarrassed and for an instant I blushed. I may be an older female at this point in my human life versus the young man in the ancient past, but I was not too old to appreciate his handsomeness.

Thoth caught my blush of acknowledgement and appreciation, winked, and couldn't control the smile emerging on his face as we hugged for the first time, no longer as adult/child, god/human, or teacher/student. Now it was associate/associate or colleague/colleague. I appreciated the return of a long-lost friend who was so much more than a friend.

Abounding Abundance

After a day of rest, Thoth took me to a new location—one we hadn't visited before on my many trips to the Library and his Abode. As we walked and talked, I sensed that he was distracted or concerned about something. It wasn't anything he said or did in particular; his energy just felt "off" to me. I had never seen him like this except for the times when he would participate in "the weighing of the heart ceremonies" when an Ancient Egyptian died. For Egyptians, the heart was the source of wisdom and linked with intellect, personality, and memory. Since the heart was the key to the afterlife, it was weighed to make sure it was light and didn't weigh down travel into the afterlife.

Back then, I didn't get to see the more personable side of Thoth, only the serious side. Even so, I never thought of him as anything but kind, fair, and wise yet always in control and the master.

After traveling down a long corridor, we stopped just long enough for the Library walls to part and allow us to enter a new chamber that was large, but not several football stadiums large. It was more like a two-story distribution center warehouse, and it was filled with food.

"Yes, food," said Thoth out loud. "This is where we grow, nurture, and stockpile our food. We always have twice as much food on hand that will feed the planet for several years in case of any crisis. We protect, feed, and nurture all life from this location.

"As you can see by looking up and around, we have a seemingly endless food supply. No one or nothing will starve. Abundance abounds in this space."

As I wondered how the food was grown, harvested, and processed, he responded by saying, "By thought! Everything is created and manifested by thought. This is a concept still lost in the 21st century but will get revisited. Yes, people are involved and important to the process, but no longer for physical labor; rather people are essential for the creative process of manifestation, as well as the human aspects of operating the harvesting, packaging, and storage equipment, and then eventually delivery.

"This is the ultimate in supply chain production and management. People and their abilities are also important because of the value each brings to the universe to work. No two are alike and each comes with a spiritual, family, and community purpose and their individual connection to our Creator.

"Humankind is the Creator's most precious creation. Our Creator, God, First Source is part of each of us, just as much as we are each a part of the Creator. Like the individual raindrop becomes part of the mighty Nile, the mighty Nile is that drop of rain along with all the other previous drops of rain. You can't have one without the other.

"Collectively, we are humanity, but humanity is made up of diverse humans. Diversity is humanity."

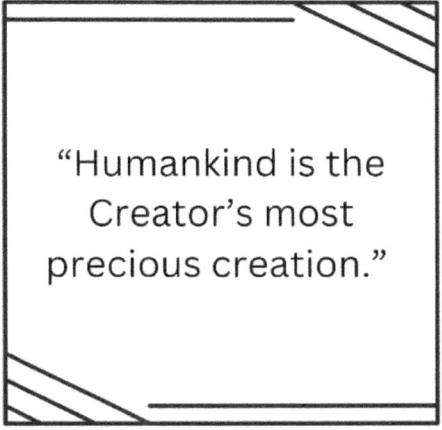

For a moment I thought Thoth had stepped up on the proverbial soapbox when my thought process was stopped in its tracks as Thoth whispered, "Ha-ha," and encouraged me to keep up.

We moved in and out of the rows of shelving where food was categorized much like a library. As we walked, I noticed that he was wearing his ibis headdress again.

We continued into another room where food was being air dried as a form of preservation. Thoth told me.

"We only use fresh or air-dried foods to preserve the most nutrients. A healthy humanity must have healthy, nourishing food to be at peak performance. We do not wish for any human to operate at any level but their best. People cannot thrive if they are supplied with food that only provides survival energy instead of maximum energy for thriving.

"The 21st century will reveal much about food and wellbeing. It will be one of several categories to receive exponential growth.

"There is one final area to cover."

Thoth's demeanor had completely relaxed by the time we entered the next room in this chamber. In fact, confidence replaced concern. As we stepped into the new area the lights were dimmed and all I saw was a spotlight shining on a pedestal table in the middle of the room. On the table was what looked like a cake. Perhaps it was someone's birthday, anniversary, or for a wedding. But since I hadn't seen any people up until now, none of those options seemed to fit the bill.

In the blink of an eye, hundreds of tiny lights appeared like sparklers and lit up the room with lots of laughter and cheering. Thoth arranged a celebration to honor our reunion after thousands of years. Food, music, and people filled the room, making it overflow with joy and love. I felt much appreciation for the thoughtful act.

An Early Wakeup

That night I fell into a deep and regenerative sleep. In the morning, I woke earlier than usual and felt overwhelmingly grateful, with deep appreciation for all I had experienced over the past few days. As I continued to reflect, I found myself reduced to tears and became sort of a malleable puddle of clay. There was something incredibly honest and beautiful about my surroundings and the celebration the evening before.

At that moment Thoth uttered the words, "Love. Unconditional love is what you are experiencing here. Where there is truth and wisdom, love prospers. Here you find the purest form of unadulterated love, which breaks down all walls and barriers. So, what you have left is the amazingly beautiful energy of pure love."

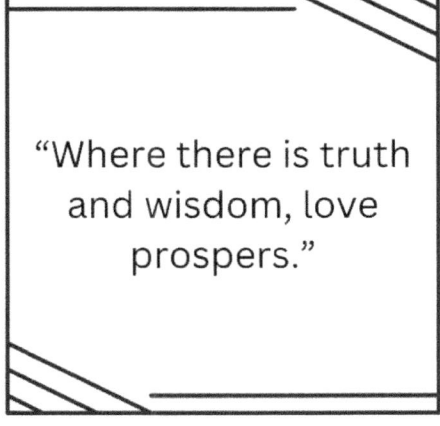

I felt the grin on his face as he said, "Un-puddle yourself and come, eat, and drink. We have another busy day in front of us. We have much to do before you are fully prepared for the journey ahead. There is still so much to see and to share. Our new journey together is just beginning."

Once I saw him, I thought that our journey for the day must be unusual because he was without his headdress. I was still having difficulty getting used to seeing his face. The time we spent together in Ancient Egypt was always formal and what I would call professional. There was a distinct class level of separation between us plus a god/child lowly scribe relationship. If there was anything else, I never felt it or saw it with Thoth. There was only a mutual respect.

He seemed a bit mischievous this day. I never saw this side of him let alone his face. He had a wonderful personality and he was right; his Abode and the Library in general were filled with over-flowing love. This was the only time I had experienced such love. It was so intense that the feeling could make you weak in the knees in one instant and fly to the mountain top in another.

Thoth interrupted my thoughts when he asked, "Are you floating on the clouds again? Isn't it a magnificent view? Go there often; it serves you well. In fact, it would serve humanity well to spend more time rejoicing on the mountains tops rather than in the dungeons of chaos and fear. Come, we must leave."

I was so caught up in the moment that I barely had time to take a bite or drink anything when off we went. Another adventure awaited us.

Doors opened and closed, but this time we turned to the right and went past Thoth's Abode. We never traveled this way before, which made it a bit unusual. But what was really different was that this time he went without his headdress.

Thoth glanced at me, as if reassuring me that all was well. This journey seemed much shorter than the others. The Library walls opened and closed quickly behind us. As my eyes acclimated to the bright sun and the great outdoors, I was shocked to see a park in front of me. How did he do this? Were we still underground? It was a park the size of New York's Central Park with flower gardens that looked like they belonged in a Monet painting, tulips as far as the eyes could see like in the Keukenhof Gardens in Holland in the spring, and roses from the Princess Grace Rose Garden in Monaco.

We strolled for hours enjoying the peace, quiet, and beauty. Gently curving through this enormous garden was a meandering stream with an occasional waterfall. Up ahead the stream fed into a peaceful lake with an island in the center that had just a bit of a land connection in the middle that formed the infinity symbol.

Thoth spoke, "This garden is a tribute to our eternal Creator. It is filled with God's desire to have every human know that they are unique, one-of-a-kind, and loved. Would you like to go to the island?"

I no more than nodded my head yes and a silent boat, or more like a floating vehicle, appeared with two seats and a table filled with refreshments. The canopy overhead offered us a bit of relief from the bright sun, although in every other way the weather was a perfect temperature with a soft breeze flowing.

We did not go directly to the island, but rather took a leisurely ride on the lake and up and down all the hidden canals. As before, one was more beautiful than the other.

We finally arrived at the island and crossed a Monetesque bridge at the center of the infinity connection. We walked to the right where a granite foot path led us to a marble labyrinth, carefully and precisely built into the lush grass.

My face must have been beaming with delight when Thoth said, "I knew you would be pleased. Come, let's walk."

We both acknowledged the presence of the Creator in this mini-Garden of Eden before we each began our journey inward. When we each arrived at the center of the labyrinth, we sat on a bench in quiet meditation and shared quiet thought. At that moment it felt like we were in the presence of our Creator God with love raining down on us. No matter how hard I tried to put my feelings into words, I couldn't. The experience was that powerful.

Without a word, we arose and slowly finished the labyrinth walk. We said our goodbyes to the island and returned to our water transportation vehicle. We took one more turn around the lake, revisiting my favorite gardens before stepping ashore in the main area of the park.

As I reflected on the day and our short walk, I kept thinking, "How could we be in such a magnificent park when we are underground and it's nighttime where my human home is located?"

Thoth leaned closer and said, "Manifestation. It's all about manifesting what brings you peace and joy on Earth."

As a footnote to the day, Thoth spoke to me about a human health need I was facing and said, "Manifest what you want to experience, how you want to feel, and the outcome. Remember our park journey filled with joy as your example. You will be at peace and love will be your companion."

I expressed my humble gratitude for his encouragement in what I was experiencing and worried about as a human. I was very grateful.

Impending Surgery in the Human World

Thoth quietly smiled at me over our first meal the next morning, knowing that as a human I was a bit, maybe a lot, uncomfortable with the eminent eye surgery I was scheduled to have. Such procedures no longer existed in his world, as it was all taken care of through prevention. Therefore, there were no invasive measures used on the body in Thoth's world, as well as no pre-op procedures or post-op after care.

Even though we were still hundreds of feet below ground, he knew my thoughts were with the human side of my life above ground. He spoke, "Be present and manifest the kind of day you wish to see. A successful surgery, back home holding your dog Crystal, and peacefully resting. All is and will be well."

As I reflected on his words and acknowledgement of my human life dog Crystal, he said "All is well and will be well. It is time to leave. We have work to do." As he spoke, I noticed he was wearing his headdress. Just then, the doors opened into the Library corridor and he moved us along on our merry way, further down the corridor to the right, well past the area where we entered the huge park. I thought we'd never get to where we were going. As usual, the second that thought occurred, we stopped, looked left, and another area of the Library wall opened, revealing what appeared to be a silent classroom.

This was the first time I saw people doing anything, except for the anniversary party. There appeared to be hundreds of students of all ages sitting classroom style at the tables, looking at screens suspended at face height in midair.

Their concentration abilities were like well-tuned audio equipment as they didn't look at us as we entered the room, nor did they look at each other when something on a screen made someone laugh.

Thoth explained, "Children learn best together as a mixed-age group. It takes away the fear of the unknown for the young ones and gives a sense of responsibility to the older ones. When there are group discussions, all ages participate, which accelerates the learning curve for the younger students, some of whom are advanced by several layers ahead of their older peers in certain fields of study.

"Prior to beginning their quest for knowledge and wisdom, all children go through a course of meditation, studying various methods so they can choose what feels right for them. They then practice meditating so they learn to take control of their minds and bodies. They are also advanced in the field of silence and self-control at an early age. Silence is an art form that humans haven't considered as a class or something children should learn to do. But silence forces people to go within and find peace, to concentrate better, and to always be in self-control.

"Children get regular breaks from the educational process, which relieves them of any pressure they might experience with such deep concentration. The break becomes more of a social interaction time, a time to visit and catch up before returning to their studies.

"Their educational experience is carefully balanced so they get just as much creativity time as logical time. The students are more at peace when balanced. It is truly amazing to watch their development as their true inner self and inner gifts blossom when in creativity time."

"What do they do for creativity," I asked. "Is it just the arts and music?"

"Creativity time can be quite varied, but it's never on the computer. Even topics like graphic arts done on the computer are a form of logical art, not creative. Children have a wide choice of creative arts other than the obvious such as painting, dancing, and sculpting. They include bird watching, candle making, weaving, a variety of yarn and beading techniques, pencil art, cooking, baking, fashion design, house décor design, and so much more. Their educational programs are very important to ensure balance yet also provide a wide variety of creative experiences.

"At the day's end, which coincides with at least one of the parents' work schedules, the children return home without any homework so they can fully participate in the family experience and help with housework and chores.

"Families are encouraged to participate in quiet time and together time before retiring for the day. In the morning they are expected to spend time in meditation, preparing both children and self to have a peace-filled and productive day.

"Humanity does not yet understand the importance of each child. But their children are the future of the country and the planet. If they are not taught responsibility for others and the planet, and how to feed, nourish, and nurture each other, how will the planet survive?"

A Few Days of Rest

Several days passed since my surgery. My family stayed with me to help during the recovery period. For the most part, the pre-surgery was the most stressful, but once I received the anesthetic, I was totally out until they woke me and told me it was time to go home. I was so grateful the surgery went well and for Thoth's encouraging words about manifesting the perfect outcome.

After a few days of rest, I was finally back with Thoth, who encouraged me to continue to rest, knowing that my human self just went through a traumatic experience. In fact, he insisted I sleep a bit longer to allow my body to recuperate. I did get up a bit later but did not notice any discomfort or tiredness—just a strange sensation that something was different. I went to the table to join Thoth for a meal.

"Your surgery went well," said Thoth. "I was there overseeing the surgeon and his team. He is a very good surgeon and took great care of you. He worked quickly and efficiently considering how unadvanced they are with their methodology compared to what will be available in the foreseeable future.

"While you had no way of knowing, my energy field totally wrapped your body with a protective healing energy blanket so no harm could touch you and only success and healing energy could permeate your body.

"Now it is time to heal your complete body." He motioned for me to follow him as he stepped out into the corridor. We arrived at the Healing Chamber, which surprised me. He told me to lay down on one of their healing beds. He then passed his hand over my body from the top of my head to the bottom of my toes. This instantly dropped me into a very deep sleep that lasted for hours.

I awoke as quickly as I fell asleep. The canopy of the bed was closed. Slowly, the canopy slid open and I saw Thoth standing beside me, just as I remembered him before going to sleep. I wondered how long I had been in there and whether Thoth was by my side all that time.

He spoke, "Yes, I have been by your side every second should you have needed me. Your session lasted five hours and fifteen minutes—the exact length of time necessary to repair past medical procedures, as well as cleanse your body of all toxins from foods, air, water, vaccinations, metal impurities, and any unresolved health issues you've been struggling with, including any physical or mental harm done by others.

"Additionally, you needed much cellular level energy regeneration. And you were very low on physical body rejuvenation. You required some deep sleep.

"This type of intensive work requires additional rest, with only light activities for at least another three days. You will heal here. You need to be 100% so you can move forward with the large task ahead. I will be by your side to help you with that task, but it is you who will lead us forward into the new Aquarian age of wisdom, knowledge, and truth."

We slowly made our way back to the Great Hall where food and drink awaited us. He said, "Eat and drink lightly so your physical body can adapt and integrate all the changes within and without. Your face is glowing and radiant. Time spent in the bed chamber has served you well."

I wanted to ask him a million questions about the bed chamber and what was used to heal my body, but I could tell by the look on Thoth's face that this was a time for nourishment, nurturing, and rest, not a left-brain interrogation. It was simply a time to rest and bask in the glow of the energies we shared.

Manifesting

"Manifest! Manifest what you want. There is nothing standing in your way. Research no more. You know the way forward." Thoth spoke with great clarity and power in his voice as his eyes pierced my heart.

"Manifest! It's your birthright. Wait no longer. You need to do this now. If it's a miracle you seek, manifest it. If it is volunteer help you need, manifest it. If it's a book on the New York Times bestsellers list, manifest it.

"Simply sit somewhere quiet, be in silence, and see clearly what you seek. If it is in alignment with who you are and what your life mission is, it will come to you. Nothing, not even yourself, can stand in your way."

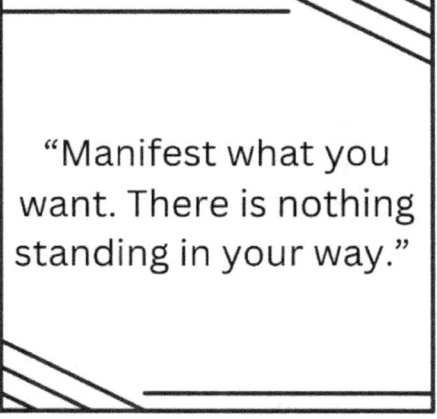

"Manifest what you want. There is nothing standing in your way."

I heard myself say out loud, "thank you," but wasn't sure where I was or even if I was awake. The acknowledgment of my gratitude resulted in a broad smile on Thoth's face, which lit up my sleeping chamber with warm welcoming sunshine. Obviously, I had been asleep when I heard Thoth's definitive voice speak with such clarity.

I arose for the day and met Thoth at the table where food and drink were served to nourish us and to heal my body. This was day two of my healing and restoration.

Since my session in the healing chamber, we hadn't gone anywhere. I assumed that this day would be spent the same way as the last. But then Thoth said, "Let's go. We are heading out for a healing experience."

As he spoke, the doors to the corridor opened quickly and quietly, as if they could read Thoth's mind. We traveled down the long corridor on some type of two-person silent hovering transport platform that we stood on while holding onto a bar in front of us for steadying purposes. It seemed to be a hybrid cross between a 21st century hover board and a Segway but it appeared to travel on air and had no wheels.

Thoth explained, "You must not compromise your healing and increased energy needs by exerting energy walking, so I ordered us transportation to ensure proper healing over the first three days. Since this is only day two, we must be careful.

"Here we are," he said as he motioned for me to get off the platform. He beckoned me to enter the beautiful flower gardens we visited once before. "The beauty and fragrance of the gardens will enhance your healing."

Another two-person floating platform showed up the instant we appeared in the garden. It took us on another adventure around the magical park. This time the focus seemed to be on the color green, although I noticed that all the groupings of flowers ranged in the colors of the chakras, including copper brown for grounding, purple for spirituality, and then white for the Creator and the universe.

Thoth responded with a twinkle in his eye, as if he was acknowledging my appreciation for the relationship of the colors to healing and balancing the chakras.

We finally reached the small infinity shaped island in the middle of the lake and walked across the bridge. On the other side was another hovering transport platform to take us to our island destination, this time the left side of the island.

Thoth spoke, "Listen. Close your eyes so you can hear." In the near distance I heard the sounds an orchestra makes when warming up before a performance. As we moved off the path out into a clearing, right before my eyes was a magnificent outdoor band shell, theater style seats, and the orchestra on stage tuning their instruments.

Thoth seemed quite pleased with himself for creating an afternoon in the park concert. The transport platform took us down to the front row center where we sat in chairs fit for royalty. However, no one else was in the audience. Overhead, gently moving in the breeze, was something like a flat tent or a quasi-roof to protect us from the sun, yet it allowed the light in.

Thoth explained, "Sound with string and wind instruments creates a healing experience for the human body, especially when you remove all other thoughts and distractions. When properly put together, music, nature, color, and fragrance are very healing for the body and mind. This is part of your healing process for today. We've spent time recalibrating your chakras and will follow that up with sound resonance."

> "When properly put together, music, nature, color, and fragrance are very healing for the body and mind."

What followed was the most magical concert I've ever experienced. Music danced off the violin strings as they played Johann Strauss II operettas and waltzes such as Die Fledermaus and the Blue Danube. Then there was the very heartfelt csárdás dance music, where the violins cried at the same time a cimbalom player's paddles danced over the open strings in Brahm's Hungarian Dance No. 5 in G minor.

The music traveled from old European and Russian favorites to more contemporary pieces like movies themes of Dr. Zhivago, Star Wars, and Indiana Jones. It was magnificent; my heart was overflowing with joy.

"Perfect," said Thoth as he looked at me. "That's exactly what I hoped for. Your whole body is glowing and your aura is radiating energy. This is a perfect healing modality for you and for all humans. Humanity responds well to the vibrational sound and frequency of string and wind instruments. This is something totally overlooked by your contemporary medicine's healing methodology.

While the process is a bit more complex than what I've explained, there are other issues involved such as composition, but the overall process is quite simple: fill the heart with joyful music and healing will take place."

Back to the Healing Chamber

The next morning, I woke up feeling rested. I walked out to the Great Hall and expected to see Thoth sitting at the table with food and drink. I glanced around the vast space of the Hall but he was nowhere in sight.

I wondered if I had lost track of time. Perhaps I missed him. I refocused and looked again toward the table. Not only was there no Thoth, but there was no food and drink present either. I was somewhere between confused and concerned.

As if on cue, the doors from the main hall opened and Thoth appeared. He motioned for me to join him. We glided down the hall on our transport platform. While it seemed like only a short trip, we traveled quite a distance back to the Healing Chamber.

I was still thinking about the food when Thoth interrupted and said, "You need more time in the healing bed chamber. While in the park yesterday, I detected a disconnected cell in you. We must reconnect it before it creates a harmful chain reaction event."

By now I was on the bed platform. I wanted to ask a million questions but I fell into a deep sleep the moment Thoth started to pass his hand over my body. Two hours and nine minutes later, I woke up at the snap of a finger. There was Thoth, right beside my bed platform, with a smile on his face. In fact, he was beaming.

As we left the Healing Chamber Thoth explained, "When we were at the concert yesterday and you were so totally relaxed, absorbing all the musical joy, I noticed a miniscule twitch near your left eye lid, which concerned me deeply. I knew I needed to see what was causing that uncontrolled motion and repair it before it became an issue. It could have been a result of the human surgery you just went through or something ancient. I know you did not have that twitch when you were my scribe in ancient times.

"I also didn't notice it when we first reunited in this lifetime. Because you have been guarded with your emotions, only once you completely relaxed when hearing the concert music did you expose the real you, including the twitch. It was a magical moment and a glimpse of your beauty within and without."

Part of me wanted to smile in appreciation of his lovely compliment, but I hid it, and he seemed nonchalant to my non-reaction. However, my blush gave me away. Thoth beamed knowing he had gotten behind my façade and touched my heart.

We arrived back at the Great Hall where food and drink awaited us. Thoth spoke, "You must nourish and nurture your body, and you must rest. This procedure requires two more days of rest, which will begin after we finish our meal. Humanity needs to understand the importance of rest and deep sleep when healing. Body cells do not respond well to multi-tasking and stress. If they are forced to do so, they will not perform any function or task well and will malfunction. Deep sleep and proper nourishment are key to having a healthy body."

The Candle

The next morning, I was sitting on a soft, comfy sofa in the Great Hall, staring into a candle as my healing time continued. At this point, I couldn't remember when I was last above ground, yet I was content doing nothing in a cave—a beautiful, wonderful, magical cave underground, so to speak—staring into a very oversized candle with one wick that produced an equally oversized flame.

Thoth was away tending to ... I didn't know exactly what ... but I assumed his Creator's work. He was away all day but his energy was very dominant in the space. I felt his presence everywhere I looked, sat, or walked, especially in the candle flame.

There was something special and unique about the essence of the candle flame. Staring at it helped my mind free itself from the human ego and settle into a natural state of third eye vision or meditation.

Thoth once told me that if a human had trouble silencing their mind for meditation or deep reflection, they should stare into the flame of a candle for several minutes and the flame would do the hard work of silencing the mind. Without silence, you cannot hear the Creator's voice.

"What have you learned?" asked Thoth as he walked into the room. I acknowledged his presence, and he asked again. "What have you learned?" I was baffled by his question but finally told him, "I can sit here in complete silence, all alone, and connect with my Creator 100% of the time. I can also connect with you in the same way should I choose to do so."

"Is there more?" he asked. "What about the candle?"

The candle? My mind scrambled for an answer when I realized the candle was a tool I or anyone could use at a moment's notice to get into quiet space. With that thought, Thoth smiled and said, "Yes. The message is clear. For those who cannot silence their mind easily or at all, the flame of a candle or a fireplace relaxes you and opens your heart instead of your mind and ego. So many people think they must go through rituals to silence their mind, but all they really need is a burning candle flame or their hand.

"To use your hand, simply flatten your hand with the fingers together, and then place the clustered fingers flat on your third eye area just above and between your eyes. Then gracefully take the same flattened hand with connected fingers and lay it over your heart."

> "For those who cannot silence their mind easily or at all, the flame of a candle or a fireplace relaxes you and opens your heart instead of your mind and ego."

"It's important that every human knows how to silence their mind. They are so distracted and congested with noise and vision pollution that they cannot connect with their Creator and hear the voice within. That's where truth and wisdom are found, not in noisy cement cities where chaos and fear reign. Humanity must wake up! They have been deliberately silenced so they can be controlled. It is their turn to become the society intended by the Creator—one where greed and indulgent self-power is destroyed and truth and love prevail."

The Importance of Balance

Thoth continued sharing his wisdom as another day began in the Great Hall. Music from the concert in the park filled the air as he carefully observed my response to the various instruments and compositions being played. I couldn't hide my joy as my mind danced to the various melodies.

Being pleased with what he observed, he said, "Come. Let's go for an outing today and continue the healing process."

We floated down the long corridor on our platform vehicle. I was about to ask how the platform functioned when he said, "It travels on energy waves radiating from the Earth. It is similar to the theory Nikola Tesla was working on before he died. People should review his teachings carefully. His wisdom and knowledge from ancient times made him a master well ahead of his time.

"Humanity took a big leap backwards during the industrial and scientific revolutions. Yes, they did simplify things and made it easier to produce items in large quantities, heal some of the sick, and travel to the moon and back. But it also stifled and stagnated generations in the muck of only one form of thought or process being allowed. If someone spoke out about science or the mass production of food, for example, or had a different opinion, they were belittled, berated, and banned from the organization.

"Once technology and science became gods, humans were no longer allowed to explore and develop other methodologies, forms of healing, manufacturing, and energy production for human use. That is what happened to Tesla. The world became a predominantly left-brain, capitalistic society with no emphasis placed on right brain activities like the arts, music, dance, color, shape, and design.

"Your current world is very lopsided and will face total imbalance until they awaken enough to re-right the ship. That is what your book, *Looking Within*, is all about—re-righting humanity so it doesn't tumble like some earlier civilizations that did not adhere to the rules of compassion, serving the people, truth, and love. Only societies based on equality, respect, and self-control, the opposite energies from science and technology, can thrive. Only balanced life honoring the energies of the planet, meeting the needs of humanity, and living life in accordance with the intent of the Creator will thrive."

> "Only societies based on equality, respect, and self-control can thrive. Only balanced life honoring the energies of the planet, meeting the needs of humanity, and living life in accordance with the intent of the Creator will thrive."

By now, we had already reached the park, floated on the lake for a while, and docked at the end of a little canal. A short walk on a narrow footpath took us to a white picturesque gazebo with a bench in the middle. It was surrounded with hundreds of roses of varying shapes, colors, and sizes. Some were miniatures and others were climbing up the gazebo corner posts, forming a prolific canopy overhead.

We sat on the bench in the quiet beauty of the day. A gentle breeze floated the fragrance of the roses, filling our senses with grace and beauty, as the warmth of the sun sang a lullaby, which allowed for deep rest and regeneration.

What Brings You Joy?

"Your memory recall is working much better and will continue to improve. You chose wisdom when you were a young mother many years ago. You understood even then that any spiritual gift you may be given or choose has little value without wisdom. Knowing what is truth and what is not, knowing when to speak and when to listen, knowing when to advise and when to step back are examples of wisdom," said Thoth.

At that moment I realized I actually heard Thoth's voice. I did not just imagine the words. He spoke again, "Rise. It's a beautiful day and there's much to do on your final day of healing." I scrambled out of bed and prepared for my day ahead. Life below ground was quite an experience. I did not long to go back to my human world above, but I did long for more and more wisdom and knowledge. My heart was far from satiated.

I moved quickly to the Great Hall. As I entered, I saw Thoth waiting for me. He greeted me with a smile, but he also had a quizzical expression on his face. It was as if he wanted to ask me something but wasn't sure of the correct approach. As we enjoyed our food and drink, he watched intently and finally spoke.

"What is your heart's desire? What do you want, need to know, or yearn to experience? You continue to be very guarded, and I see only glimpses of your true self. What brings you joy? What fills your heart with overflowing love and light?"

This question surprised me because I assumed Thoth could read my mind since we conversed silently through thought waves. Also, I didn't know the answer to his question.

Thoth interrupted my private thoughts, "When you need to totally relax and release your body and mind to the universe for restoration and regeneration, where do you go? What do you do?"

Again, I drew a blank but told him how it gives me joy when I journal and am 100% connected spiritually 100% of the time. During those times, I feel nurtured and complete, much like I felt at that moment with the two of us having meaningful conversations and sharing time. While Thoth appreciated what I said, I could tell he wasn't satisfied with my answer and wanted more.

"Come. Let's go for a ride," he said. "I have a treat for you." We traveled quickly down a corridor and then abruptly stopped in an unfamiliar area. I marveled at how this underground world of magic had never-ending possibilities. Thoth was obviously connected to my inner thoughts, as he seemed amused. As the door opened, we stepped into a shelter of sorts that was filled with hundreds of domesticated animals roaming freely in gigantic room-sized play pens. The animals were with other like-type animals: cows of all types in one pen, cats in another, dogs in yet another. It went on and on. As it turned out, this was the Unconditional Joy Chamber.

I was about to speak when my eyes returned to the front of the room. Sitting there in a row, just a couple of feet away from me, were all my pets from childhood up to the present with out-of-control wagging tails. "Oh my goodness!" I cried out.

As soon as I spoke and made eye contact with the pets, they all barreled toward me, knocking me to the floor with their excitement. They covered me with their wet kisses and fuzzy nuzzles; it was a gleeful moment. Once I re-righted myself, I was overjoyed and petted and hugged each and every one many times, including my present lifetime dog Crystal. She was a bit confused, having to share me with other animals, but then she noticed Thoth and rushed toward him. They acted like long lost buddies, which made me wonder if they had shared a lifetime together somewhere along the way, making this a reunion for them as well. Following that thought, I questioned further and wondered if he had sent Crystal to me? He was quite involved with Crystal but looked up at that moment and smiled, perhaps acknowledging my musings about him being responsible for her presence in my current life.

We spent hours in this area, moving from one pen to another. In one pen were several cows from the farm I grew up on. In another pen were various horses I loved from past lives, including the black stallion I rode lifetimes ago in the Black Forest when I was killed by robber barons as I was enroute to help a neighbor. This horse seemed particularly happy to see me alive and well, as he carried a lot of guilt and felt responsible for my death.

Nearby were the swans from the Manor in the Black Forest. I loved them and they loved my care and nurturing. I saw and spoke to one of their present generation ancestors when I visited the Black Forest several years ago in this lifetime. He was a magnificent specimen, as he left his bevy and paddled all the way across the Rhine River to get my attention and give me a message. Next to the swans in the reeds and muck was a small group of ibis. I thought of Thoth every time I saw an ibis and have done so since I was 10 years old, when I first opened that large Golden children's book filled with pictures of the Great Pyramids and all the gods, including Thoth with his ibis head.

As we neared the ibis' area, one male proudly walked directly toward me. "Oh my!" I exclaimed. I just saw this ibis in my human life a few weeks ago at a small beach-front community restaurant. He brazenly flew into the restaurant and landed on a table a few feet away from me, making sure he got my attention so he could give me his message, "I am always with you and you are healed." I would have recognized that bird as Thoth anywhere and anytime. He was magnificent as he boldly strutted toward me on that restaurant table.

Thoth spoke, "All these animals are here to thank you for your loving care. You touched each of their lives with kindness and love in their lifetimes. You reached each at the heart level and enjoyed a very deep connection.

"They are also here to remind you that one of the things that brings true joy to your life is animals, especially dogs. That was true in every lifetime, including being a young scribe in ancient times. You found joy in what you call their unconditional love. You can come here anytime to spend time with them and you will receive joy.

"What brings you the most joy is the unconditional love. Certain types of music also speak to you the with same kind of unconditional love energy. Animals, such as dogs, and certain flowers and plants with beauty and fragrance, also provide you that energy.

"Now you can reflect upon the question: What gives you joy, so much that your heart overflows? What provides you the most relaxation, refueling, and restoration? You need to know this to manifest it. All humans need to know this so they can continually refuel and restore self for peak performance."

> "What gives you joy, so much that your heart overflows? What provides you the most relaxation, refueling, and restoration?"

Gratitude and Appreciation

Another day of healing and caring for myself was underway. I never knew what to expect other than to be prepared to experience something wonderful or uplifting that would provide me glowing regenerative energy. At times, I found myself pouring through ancient manuscripts. Other times I sat in the Technology Chamber and stared at the enormous star tetrahedron as it continued its never ending revolving in the mid-section of the Chamber. It was magical as it moved in a steady counter-clockwise motion suspended from nothing and being held up by nothing. I didn't understand it, yet I found it to be truly mystical.

During each day, Thoth came and went as he continued with his work, although we always shared food and drink at least once every day. The days seemed to fly by, yet it seemed like only yesterday when he directly spoke to me for the first time in my journaling and said, "We begin…It is I, Thoth, your trusted associate." That was one of the most magical and exhilarating moments in my life. The last time I had mentioned him in my journaling was well over two years earlier. I was writing about things I wished to manifest when I asked the universe and my Creator about having direct one-on-one conversations with Thoth so I could better serve others. As I continued looking back through my journals, I found that I had made a similar request eight years earlier.

In hindsight, this manifestation took so long because my physical and mental body were not yet in alignment with my spiritual side. Alignment, change, and growth were essential for me to manifest Thoth in my life. I was so grateful that I recognized the need to spend time with Thoth, and the need to access through him the Ancient Library of Wisdom and Knowledge. I was equally grateful for the deep-seated burning desire to penetrate more deeply into my spiritual growth and alignment. This was a blessing I was deeply honored to receive and now share with others.

As I reflected on the journey it took to get here and the appreciation for the connection, the Great Hall door parted and in walked Thoth, removing his headdress. He questioned, "Were you talking about me? The sweet sounds of gratitude preceded me down the corridor into the room." I, being rather embarrassed, lowered my head so he couldn't see my cheeks turning red. He went on, "You are gracious beyond words. Everyone wants and needs to feel appreciated, at least occasionally. Appreciation is something that is lacking in modern society just as much as in ancient societies.

"Humans need acknowledgement and to feel appreciated. Those two things lead the way to respect and equality. When you acknowledge and appreciate the small things, the large things become much easier. You cannot constantly berate humans or animals and expect them to perform their best. But when you nurture and nourish them with kindness and appreciation, they will blossom and produce. Even the beautiful blue lotus flower finds nourishment in the muck of the Nile and blossoms."

> "When you nurture and nourish people with kindness and appreciation, they will blossom and produce."

Thoth was at his best when he taught without teaching. I loved this about him. Out of the simplest thought or action, he could speak for fifteen or fifty minutes without hardly taking a breath.

One day we were casually talking about the highly sought after philosopher's stone. He said, "All of the scientists in the world sought the magic of the philosopher's stone, thinking it would turn something into gold. The thing that each of them missed was that they all had the philosopher's stone within. All they had to do was go within and reconnect with their Creator. The real philosopher's stone was the unconditional and infinite love they would find when connected to their eternal One Source, God, the Creator, not fool's gold that can be lost, given away, or stolen at a moment's notice." He went on for another half hour before taking a deep breath.

> "The real philosopher's stone is the unconditional and infinite love you will find when connected to your eternal One Source, God, the Creator."

Since he always seemed to know what I was thinking, he was rather amused at my description of the conversation and finally with a grin said, "Come. Let's have food and drink and continue our conversation."

Crystal

I awoke to find my human lifetime dog Crystal snuggled up next to me. While I adored having her with me, I was confused. How could she be here in Thoth's Abode when she was currently in my human home? Or was I in my human home dreaming I was in the sleeping chamber? She was here the day we visited the Unconditional Love Chamber but went back to her human life after that experience.

Thoth's voice interrupted my thoughts as he said, "Come Crystal. Your breakfast is ready." Recognizing his voice, she jumped up in a flash and dashed to meet him. She was excited, and while that answered several questions about where I was, I still didn't know how she got here.

As we sat and enjoyed our food and drink together, I quizzed Thoth by asking about Crystal's presence. He spoke with a rather sheepish grin on his face. "She seemed very lonely with your presence manifesting so much time here at the Abode that I felt it would be in her best interest and yours if she joined us." This was so humorous that I laughed out loud as I looked at him and then her curled up by his feet. Now it was he who blushed from embarrassment as he realized I saw right through his pretense. He continued, "I, too, missed her energy. It's been many years since we were companions and it is so good to have her energy field here again." This time Crystal barked, making him acknowledge that he did send her to me and wanted her here to keep both of us company.

Thoth was still concerned about my need for additional rest, healing, and regeneration, so we spent a quiet day together. We took Crystal on a walk to the park with the many flowers and the lake. We let her run and play in the sun as we sat in the gazebo. All the wonderful fragrances from the roses refueled my energy as we watched her play tag with a rabbit and chase a squirrel up a tree.

I deeply treasured days like these because they filled me with so much joy. In some ways I wished I could live out the remainder of my life here, even though I knew I had much work to do as a human.

Thoth spoke, "Yes, I treasure the time I share with a trusted and loved colleague."

Fear and Stress

We've been up for hours moving quickly from chamber to chamber searching for Crystal. She decided to take an early stroll in the Library and was able to trigger the opening of the Great Hall's corridor door. She must have been carrying enough of both Thoth's and my energy for the door to recognize her and open. That meant other doors would also recognize her and open.

Thoth put the front entrance to the Library into lockdown mode so she couldn't escape into the desert, but we knew she could be anywhere else in the massive underground complex. One of the first places we checked was the park, as she loved it there. But there was no sign of her and she did not respond to our beckoning calls and tempting rewards of love and treats.

We moved on more quickly since she wasn't in her favorite places. Thoth monitored each chamber for movement and her energy field as our platform transported us down the various corridors. We stopped in each chamber to double check for her presence. Every doorway and every room had surveillance capabilities so he could also check camera footage to see if one little dog had passed through the mammoth door openings or if there was unusual movement in any room. But there was nothing—no sound, no movement, and nothing out of place.

Thoth was concerned about my healing and wellbeing, I was upset about Crystal, and he knew I wouldn't rest until we found her. He spoke, "Look at me. I want to scan your body to make sure all is well." He stared into my eyes deeply, as if scanning my entire body and creating a mini map of every cell in my body. I finally broke the silence because I could no longer deal with his intensive piercing stare. "Well?" I said, with the hope of getting an answer so we could continue the search.

Thoth finally spoke, "You must control your fear. It does not serve you well. Fear in humans always destroys endorphins—the neurotransmitters that help the body with pain relief and increase pleasure. This can lead to increased pain, depression, anxiety, trouble sleeping, and even addiction. You are definitely in need of laughter, listening to music, and even eating some dark chocolate.

"Come. Let's go find Crystal and get you back to the Main Hall so we can bring you back into balance. I have an idea." He whisked us down another corridor with great determination. Because he knew I was in need of an instant energy lift, we stopped by the Unconditional Joy Chamber where all my favorite animals resided.

The door opened and closed quickly behind us. Just as I was going to ask a question, Thoth pointed and said, "Look who is snuggled right in the middle of all your dogs from your past."

Right there was Crystal, sound asleep and surrounded by her new best friends. Thoth called Crystal by name. She popped up but with a guilty look on her face.

Her tail was absolutely still. She knew she did a bad thing but she also knew we would find her there and forgive her. The happy reunion started to rebuild my endorphins, which pleased Thoth.

The Scribes' Chamber

"Now that we are several days into your healing period," Thoth said, "I believe we can resume our tour around the Library. We will still travel by platform so you don't use up precious healing energy in the process of getting to the experience. The transport vehicle is just outside the door waiting for us. Let's go."

Off we went headed toward the Library's entrance. This surprised me since we rarely traveled in the direction of the hall cross. We neared the cross section; the platform didn't turn left or right but instead headed straight across the intersection and down the corridor. The platform appeared to have only one steady speed, as if its only intent was to get us to our next destination safely, not necessarily speedily. The platform stopped in front of the Library walls. A section of the Library walls moved forward and then sideways, revealing another oversized room. This room looked vaguely familiar.

Thoth spoke, "This is the Scribes' Chamber and depicts the many varieties of spoken and written words throughout the millennia. You will see the writers' and artisans' depictions of stories recorded on the walls by cave dwellers. Closer to us are much more sophisticated sculpted pictures on walls. This is the type of work you did with me in Ancient Egypt. You were extremely good at what you did and I could always depend on you and trust you with my greatest secrets." I thought to myself, *what an honor to have served the Great Thoth and have him acknowledge me.*

"As we move on, you can see great examples of scribes and their work right up until the invention of the printing press, typewriters, computers, motion pictures, and cell phones."

I turned my attention to Thoth. I realized his mouth was not moving when he spoke and he was communicating via brain waves. That surprised me because it seemed as if we were having a verbal conversation.

Thoth simply winked and continued, silently. "In many of the early compositions, the scribes recorded what others told them to write. As the years passed, scribes moved from recording to a more creative mode, realizing that they could record their own version of events and thoughts. Or they could even create new thoughts and ideas and record them instead just repeating or recording history or differing versions of other's stories.

"This is where and when words became particularly important. This is also the time when these new creator scribes discovered that they could impact the lives of others by their word choices. They could move people into a state of fear and tears, joy and happiness, love or hate, and belief or disbelief.

"Once the motion picture or a video was added to those words, the creator scribes realized they could affect entire societies.

"The same was true for writing speeches and educational books. Words of politicians and teachers using the new written materials could change the direction of entire civilizations.

"Humanity does not understand the impact of words used by others. Nor do they understand the full impact of words they say to themselves within their own minds. Just as societies can be driven into war with the use of specific words, so can a person drive themselves into defeat before they even begin."

I touched Thoth's arm and out loud said, "Breathe." Thoth stopped and realized he'd been carrying on for quite some time. A bit sheepishly he said, "Soapbox?" I cracked a little smile. He suggested we rest and have food and drink so I could maintain my energy. We sat and partook in pleasant conversation while we ate and drank so I could clear my head and rest.

> "Just as societies can be driven into war with the use of specific words, so can a person drive themselves into defeat before they even begin."

Some of my favorite music began to play in the background, almost putting me in a trancelike state. Looking back, he likely did that deliberately so I could shut my mind off for a few minutes and get some rest. However, he probably also needed the music to do the same. His passion for the use and abuse of words could pierce the heart of any listener, reader, or viewer. It was as if he was sending flares up high in the night sky to make all humanity aware of the danger in words when hollow and deceitful, not including truth, wisdom, peace, and love.

The music stopped and Thoth asked "Have you rested? Are you ready to move on?" Barely giving me enough time to nod my head yes, he headed off toward the corridor door and beckoned me to come. "The platform vehicle awaits," he said. "We will continue this conversation back in the Great Hall."

Almost as if Thoth preprogrammed the vehicle, it took off slowly then moved into something like warp speed. We were back in front of the door to the Abode in an instant. It reminded me of scenes from Star Wars where they would move at warp speed to reach another galaxy or evade capture by the dark side.

Words Matter

Thoth began this morning where he left off yesterday afternoon. "Words matter. Words create everything in your life and in the universe. Use words that are encouraging, uplifting, and empowering at all times. You can't create something good, powerful, uplifting, and joyful from negative words and thoughts. You can't create or manifest a better life if you are focused on the negative. No matter how hard you try, you cannot attract something good from something bad."

> "Use words that are encouraging, uplifting, and empowering at all times. You can't create something good, powerful, uplifting, and joyful from negative words and thoughts."

"Humanity must reprogram itself and work with the language of the heart, not the head. The heart knows only of love, light, and joy. It will lead you to your highest good because it is connected to your Creator. It always has been and will always be.

"Humanity must cast off the negativity implanted in their minds by others, including family members, society, and peers, and seek the truth within. That is the only way they can become a better, more loving, and connected human.

"So many nations and civilizations fall because of following unwise, greedy, controlling leaders. The collapse of nations is a cycle that can and must be stopped so humanity can move forward. Each and every human has an opportunity to choose the use of positive or negative thinking and the outward expression of those thoughts.

"If your thoughts are in your highest and best interest and bring no harm to others, then you are on the right path. If you are constantly putting yourself and others down, stop and think about how you are destroying yourself and perhaps others as well.

"Adults do this to themselves all the time. Even worse, they do it to their children and their co-workers all the time too."

> "If your thoughts are in your highest and best interest and bring no harm to others, then you are on the right path. If you are constantly putting yourself and others down, stop and think about how you are destroying yourself and perhaps others as well."

I finally caught Thoth's eye and he realized he should take a few deep breaths and drink something before speaking again. His passion was so deep and singularly focused, almost as if his image on the ancient Egyptian tomb walls finally had the opportunity to step off into real life and lay bare his heart. While his image is most often depicted as an ibis or baboon, it was truly a silent image with no way for him to verbally express his wisdom and knowledge to future generations.

The wisdom of this ancient god was awe-inspiring, yet little to none of it was recorded on the pyramid walls or papyrus rolls that spoke of his eloquence and intense desire to pass on his wisdom and knowledge through antiquity to those who could hear his voice.

Thoth very kindly and quietly thanked me for intently listening and for acknowledging his need to speak to a whole new generation in a civilization's cycle that is in trouble.

He said, "It pains me greatly to see humans waste a lifetime on fear and lack of fulfillment when by their own choice they could reach for the stars and find joy, peace, and happiness. So much rests on their choice of words. So many times, they choose words that destroy their very essence and feeds on all the negativity of others and what the world throws their way.

"Each and every human has been given the gift of life and the freedom of choice. It is their birth right to be successful and live a fulfilled life of peace and joy. Choose words that fulfill the Creator's birth right gift and blessing. You are a success or failure based upon the words you choose."

A Long Distance Trip

I exchanged morning greetings with Thoth. He arrived in the Great Hall before me and sat at the table with Crystal happily cradled in his lap. He asked me how I was feeling. My response was a non-committal "okay." He scowled, to which I responded, "I am feeling a bit better each day. Thank you for asking."

As Crystal snuggled more deeply into Thoth's strong arms that were lovingly holding her, he woke her with his booming voice as he said, "Good! The two of us are off on an adventure today, ending with a spectacular dinner for two under the stars."

Crystal was not happy about being relegated to staying home, but Thoth reassured her that she would be well cared for and would have plenty of play time to share with her friends in the Unconditional Joy Chamber where all my past dogs, animals, and birds lived.

"Another adventure begins!" Thoth said. First, we are traveling, and then we will dine. I've already made the necessary preparations. Our transportation awaits us."

After saying our goodbyes to Crystal, we left the Grand Hall. To my surprise, a two-person transport capsule from the Transportation Center was waiting to take us to the large transport area. We transferred unnoticed to a larger capsule where Thoth keyed in the destination's location and said, "Sit. We have a long journey ahead.

"As we leave the Library Complex and rise into the atmosphere, we will not be detected due to our sophisticated equipment. We will head west at a quickened speed, but not warp speed as you would describe it. We will be traveling several thousand miles so sit back and relax. In fact, let's move to the conversation area where snacks and drink await us."

The inside of the capsule surprised me as it was quite large and comfortable. We headed to the conversation center, which was more like a dining area with a table, chairs, and a buffet-like serving area. Beyond that were two smaller rooms, one for exercise and the other for business use or quiet regeneration and meditation. At the far end were two personal hygiene and dressing areas. I noticed Thoth's belongings in one and some of my things, including extra clothing, in the other. I was a bit taken aback and wondered why I needed additional clothing and where we were going.

Thoth motioned for me to sit and then spoke, "This is a wonderful transportation vehicle for traveling longer distances. Humanity will receive the knowledge for creating such vehicles only when they escape from the current strangle hold of the greed-driven mega corporations controlling the fossil fuel industry. The information is out there and readily available but continues to be buried by those in control. There are no negative noise or air pollutions issues, plus no fossil fuel consumption. The people and the environment are protected.

"Have some food and drink; time will pass quickly. In fact, we are already half way there."

We enjoyed small talk while we ate and drank. As we neared our destination, the sun started to rise, but all I could see below was water, lots of water, so I assumed we were heading to America. It turned out that I was ever so slightly right, but still wrong. We rapidly approached the southern-most tip of South America and then turned a bit to the right. There, straight ahead of us, was Antarctica, one of my favorite places of intrigue.

Much to my shock, it was green and lush with high mountains, waterfalls, streams, and wildlife. As I gasped at its beauty and revelation, Thoth told me, "This is what is known today as Antarctica, a frozen wasteland where penguins and researchers from several countries live. I wanted you to see what ancient history looked like when Atlantis sank. As you see, life is everywhere. There is no ice. It was a tropical paradise in the middle of the Atlantic Ocean between Africa on the east and South America on the west. When a meteor struck planet Earth thousands of years ago near the equator of the Americas, all land masses were moved and thrown into massive chaos. Water levels changed, the polar axis changed, and planet Earth was dark for many years. The animals and plants were instantly flash frozen or fried to a crisp.

"I wanted you to experience and see with your own eyes what this magnificent land mass looked like before the meteor catastrophe. We will travel at a slower speed and much lower altitude so you can see the entire continent."

I took in all the beauty of this amazing reality. I saw massive mountains that jutted thousands of feet up into the sky, long flowing rivers like the Nile, and fresh water lakes sprinkled everywhere.

On the northern side of the continent I saw tropical vegetation, but not like a jungle; the center section seemed more like the middle of the United States or southern Europe. I speculated that it was the summer season, as there were field-like patches of wildflowers but no flowering trees in sight.

The southern side seemed more barren and browner, indicating perhaps it was much colder there. It also appeared to have many deep gorges and caverns. Today, in my human world, there is so much secrecy by various governments about the central part of the continent that it is blurred out by 21st century computer search engines so humanity cannot see it in the modern world.

We spent several more hours swooping back and forth over the majestic beauty of this continent, soaking in all it stood for and had to offer, now covered with miles of ice and buried fresh water lakes.

With a sigh, Thoth spoke, "Someday, this continent will not be such a mystery and will give up its many secrets. But now, we must leave and venture home so we can dine. Our beds have been readied for sleep while we travel. Enjoy your dreams about what lies ahead."

Dining Under the Stars

As I awoke, I felt our transport vehicle drop in altitude and speed. I also heard Thoth's voice, "Arise and get dressed. Dinner will be waiting upon our arrival. Special clothing was created just for this evening. It awaits you in your dressing chamber."

Thoth was again communicating in brain waves as he was nowhere to be seen and his sleeping area was already transformed back into his travel seat. I hurried off to my dressing chamber where an assistant was waiting for me, sort of like a lady in waiting would be in a royal household. She scurried around, helping me where she could, and then brought me special clothing to wear. Strangely, I felt a bit like a princess.

She helped me into a natural linen colored dress that descended to my ankles. I thought it looked lovely, simple, and elegant. Next, she sat me down, curled my hair into an updo, and applied makeup so I looked ever so slightly like the beautiful queen Nefertiti. Fortunately, she stopped on her own before I had to prevent her from creating a full-blown Cleopatra movie set look.

Just when I thought I was done, she motioned for me to come. There was more. She placed a royal blue silk sash over my head, onto my left shoulder, and pulled it loosely together on the right side below the waist, securing it with a large gold pin with a raised lotus flower sculpted onto the rough gold background. The sash had a gold silk cord edging finishing the full length of the sash on both sides as it fell to my ankles. The gold pin glistened and set the entire look ablaze. The blue sash turned a lovely dress into a stunning look. Next, she placed a gold cuff bracelet on my left wrist, and then my right wrist. Each bracelet was sculpted with alternating lotus flowers and ibis. The last thing she placed on me was a necklace of blue lapis gemstones being held between two gold lotus flowers. The design repeated itself around my neck and was quite stunning. The ensemble of clothing and jewelry plus the lapis blue colored sandals on my feet created majestically simple yet stunning fashion.

Thoth called my name as our transportation vehicle came to a stop. "Are you ready? We've arrived." I stepped into the main seating area. Thoth stood near the door waiting for me. I gasped almost out loud at his handsomeness. I guess I never totally looked at him as a man. I've always thought of him as an Egyptian god in an ibis headdress when I knew him as a young man. Yes, he did remove his headdress most of the time in private, but I never directly looked at him. Mostly, we sat side-by-side talking, because that allowed for in-depth conversation without emotion.

Thoth was dressed in clothing similar to mine: All-natural colored linen with a tunic style shirt that had sleeves to the elbows and matching pants. He had the same blue sash tied around his shirt at the waist and blue sandals. He wore two gold arm cuffs on each lower arm, one near the wrist and one near the elbow. Each cuff had raised sculpted ibis in the gold. His necklace was similar to mine yet much more rugged and bold looking. He really was handsome.

"Come, we must go," he said. "They're waiting for us." His blushed slightly. I'm sure he enjoyed my awkwardness and nonverbal compliment. He continued, "You look lovely in your Ancient Egyptian evening wear. It suits you perfectly. Simple yet elegant."

We stepped out of the vehicle and stood under the star lit sky. I saw that we were back at the large park I loved. The air was heavy with the fragrance of roses, so I guessed we were heading to the gazebo. Candle light gave the foot path just enough illumination to make the short walk enjoyable and safe. As we stepped into the clearing, I saw the gazebo dressed in its finest evening attire of glimmering tiny lights and flickering candles. It was oozing with charm and elegance.

I gave Thoth a more than quizzical look questioning what this was all about. He responded by saying, "Let's dine. Tonight is about pure pleasure, taking care of you, and taking care of me. Humans are so busy doing the unimportant that they forget the important. They forget to care for those they love, including themselves, and to find their joy in life."

> "Humans are so busy doing the unimportant that they forget the important. They forget to care for those they love, including themselves, and to find their joy in life."

"Joy can be found in the smallest rose bush to the largest piece of quarried marble, from a beautifully polished piece of lapis jewelry to a puppy eagerly wagging its tail. Humans have given up these moments of joy in return for spending endless hours of time on their electronic gadgets and big screen televisions instead of sharing their time with loved ones, friends, and neighbors.

"Perhaps even more important, they block the connection they have with their Creator, the ultimate giver of joy.

"When was the last time you sat outside under the starlight and enjoyed a quiet dinner, for one, two, or however many gathered? It is an awe-inspiring experience.

"Come. Let's dine and enjoy the light show designed by the original Creator. We will enjoy good food, beverage, and music under the stars because it is good for us. It honors our beings and our Creator."

As we dined and enjoyed our beverage, a small string quartet somewhere in the background played and the stars above performed like magic. It was beauty to behold, and magical to experience.

Appreciation

I awoke the next morning back in the Abode after what seemed more like a short nap than a full night's rest. My mind was still overflowing with joy from the wonderful evening Thoth created to emphasize the importance of joy in every human life.

Thoth was often thought of as a magician. If true, last evening was a fine example of his expertise. I walked into the Great Hall where he sat reading something that looked like a transparent newspaper hanging in the air at eye level in front of him. He looked up as I entered and said, "You are still glowing from our joy-filled adventure last evening. It is written all over your face. Joy is a very good look for you; it serves you well. I see you are still wearing one of the wrist bands. I am honored. It is a gift for fulfilling your promise to return and unseal the lock to the Library of Wisdom and Knowledge. In fact, the entire ensemble you wore last night is yours. You will need it again in the not-so-distant future."

Trying to interrupt so I could graciously thank him for the entire experience, including the abundance of joy in my heart, became a futile exercise as he continued, "I know. I can see the gratitude and joy in your eyes and feel your great appreciation in your heart. You are welcome.

Gratitude and appreciation are noble gifts you can give to anyone for even the smallest kindness.

"The more you can show and express your gratitude for all things, large or small, the faster the world will heal and the quicker humanity will be able to live in peace and harmony. People need to respect and honor equality in others and maintain self-control before they will find peace. Societies as a whole need to respect and honor other societies before peace can reign in a nation. And nations need to do the same before peace can engulf the world.

"And it all begins with the smallest of kind gestures and acts of appreciation. The more one expresses appreciation and gratitude, the more one is given. It is like the movement of a pendulum. The more you grow your appreciation on the swing one way, the more you manifest or create positive things on the swing in the other direction. Or, you can also use the scales of justice as an example. The more gratitude you place on one side, to maintain balance, the more you manifest or are given on the other side."

> "The more you can show and express your gratitude for all things, large or small, the faster the world will heal and the quicker humanity will be able to live in peace and harmony."

He stopped abruptly as if in mid-thought, which did finally give me the opportunity to express my gratitude properly and tell him how special it was to not only see pre-historic Antarctica but also how honored I was to enjoy such majesty and beauty in the rose garden of the park. It was an awe-inspiring picture of peace and joy permanently etched in my heart to enjoy at a moment's notice.

He may have intended the evening to be a learning experience or a "how to" visual example of the ultimate creation of joy, but it honored me more deeply than that. He knew me well enough in this lifetime we've shared together so far to create the perfect joy experience for me. For others, it may be camping on the top of a mountain, having a massage on the beach, or a movie night with popcorn. But for me, it was the perfect evening, a complete immersion experience of joy.

God that Maintains the Universe

Thoth went back to observing his transparent screen, explaining that one of his responsibilities was to monitor and oversee the energy of the universe and its various galaxies. The screen was downloading information from each galaxy and he in turn was mentally aggregating all that information to determine how it would impact the energy flow of the universe as a whole.

I was more than impressed. I should have known he had this duty, because in Ancient Egypt Thoth was often referred to by several god titles, including god of the moon, god of wisdom and knowledge, god of art and writing, god of magic, and god of concepts of order and justice. But I never quite understood as a young scribe what it meant when someone described him as the god that maintained the universe.

My mind raced as I thought of his greatness and importance in our vast universe, including in the 21st century. Then to reconcile his vast importance to the fact that here I sat, in his presence, and was being treated like a long-lost dear friend placed upon a queen-like pedestal.

I tried to wrap my head around this mere mortal concept when Thoth spoke, "You are no mere mortal. You have chosen to reunite with me as we agreed so many millennia ago. You have chosen to reunite with our Creator God, the First Source of Energy. You are a divinely guided being who was chosen for this lifetime to bring forth a message of hope, peace, and joy.

"Every human is born with a purpose. Most ignore it, might not know it even exists, or put it off until late in life when they are no longer able to complete their purpose. They don't realize how important they are to their Creator—the One who is in constant contact with them. Yet people ignore the whispers, messages, and synchronicities of events in their lives. They are too busy worshipping their electronic toys, the tainted words of their puppeteer leaders, biased news media programs, money, and greed. They are totally out of balance with little harmony in their lives and no joy.

"But people like you, who have remembered who you are and have chosen to follow the path of light, vocally encourage people of their need for higher connection. You remind them that they are eternally connected to their Creator and have never been disconnected by their Creator. It is humanity that has done the disconnecting. Your Creator has created within each being in the 21st century the desire to bring about hope, peace, and joy on planet Earth."

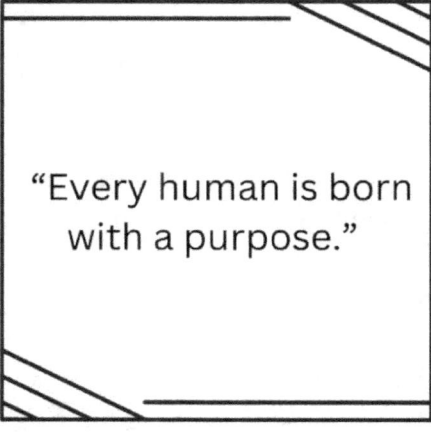

"Every human is born with a purpose."

"Every person is a much-loved child of the Creator God and is given a special job to perform while on Earth. Every task is equally important; one is not better or more important that the other. Only the human mind and others trying to control you for their gain could be that divisive, trying to undermine your greatness.

"With each breath you take, you encourage individuals to re-connect with their Creator, bask in the Creator's energy and love, and respond to God's beckoning call of eternal connection and fulfillment of your life commitment. It will serve you well and help humanity move closer to realizing hope, peace, and joy."

A Lengthy Trip

As Thoth continued receiving the download of information from each galaxy, he abruptly stopped the download, concentrating very intensely on one section and dissecting the information from one of the seven galaxies.

As abruptly as he stopped, he started again and finally spoke as he finished his review. "We need to take a trip, a lengthy trip. I need to experience in person what is happening in Galaxy 6. I sense a disturbance there not addressed in their download. We will travel three days before arriving, so plan three days there and then a three-day return.

"Our belongings, food, and water are being loaded on our long-distance transport as I speak and will be readied for travel by the time we eat our evening meal. We will be traveling at great speed so there will not be much to see until we've left the Milky Way. Then we will stop and wait almost a day simply floating in space until Galaxy 6 revolves to its closet point. We will travel again at very high speed and arrive in Galaxy 6 approximately midday so I can begin my evaluation process in the Chamber of the Presiding Leadership. I wish you to stay aboard our vehicle until I return later in the day. I have activated all the cameras in the city scape including the one that will show you where I am at all times. Should you need anything or be afraid, simply touch that screen and I will respond immediately."

After our evening meal we said goodbye to Crystal and embarked on our journey, which played out exactly as Thoth described. Sleeping, eating, and conversation were abundant. And he was right about not seeing much. After we hung out in the universe for a day, Thoth cautioned, "Do not go outside the vehicle or eat anything not provided on the vehicle when we are there. Although the inhabitants look similar to human lifeform and are friendly and accepting of outsiders, their eco system is very different than on planet Earth and could do great harm to your internal digestive system.

"You will enjoy watching them as they are quite harmonious and industrious. And their children are adorable, fun-loving, and very teachable. In some ways, it might feel like you are living a Sci-Fi movie."

The vehicle stopped and Thoth announced, "We are here, docked, and ready to disembark. Our vehicle is secure and being readied for our return home."

At that point, Thoth left the vehicle. A rowdy crowd raucously greeted him. He looked magnificent in his ibis headdress, and it was obvious the crowds loved him and had seen him before on more than one occasion. They cheered him as he entered a vehicle that seemed like a throwback to the Jetson's car from the 1960's sitcom about an automated push button world of the future.

The local population knew he was coming. I excitedly watched the streets that were lined with adoring fans and admirers. Thoth arrived at their Chamber of Leadership where the architecture looked futuristic and held a slight resemblance to the Taj Mahal and other onion domed buildings.

Again, the huge crowds cheered him on as he left the vehicle through an enclosed canopied walkway and entered the Chamber of Leadership. While keeping an eye on Thoth's camera screen, I also looked at the many other screens I wasn't aware of until he opened them. They were all hiding in plain site on a blank wall in the main cabin. They were visible only when he activated them. I questioned mentally whether they could all be made into one big screen, and instantly all the individual screens switched to the one massive screen focused on Thoth. Apparently, he programmed the screens to be thought sensitive to me as well. Or, maybe our energies were so much in harmony that the screen responded energetically as if he were present.

I quickly reversed the process back to the small screens, keeping one eye on Thoth. His sessions seemed to be going well so I started observing the local population.

They did resemble humans but their eyers were much larger. They had hands and arms, legs and feet, but their bodies were more like vertical rectangles. Think of the boxy square look of a Lego person who is tall. They had broad smiles and smiled a lot in their day-to-day activities. This day seemed to be a holiday as children played outside with no technology toys in sight.

My eye was quickly drawn to Thoth's screen again as I saw him rise and give the Leadership a farewell greeting with a nod of the head and his right hand over his heart. It seemed too early for his return. Perhaps he was headed somewhere else.

I followed his movements. Much of the crowd from earlier had dissipated but those who were left cheered as he passed by.

He spoke to me through brain waves, "I'm heading back to the vehicle but need to make one brief stop along the way. I will see you in a few minutes. In the meanwhile, we've been invited to a dinner party at the Grand

Chamber. Your evening wear has been readied for our celebratory evening.

The Dinner Party

As I headed back to my dressing chamber, I wondered what type of event was considered a celebration on this unfamiliar 6th Galaxy planet. Then I saw my dress hanging in my dressing room. It was a magnificent ball gown in shimmering black with tiny flecks of gold throughout. Below was a pair of gold sandals. Just as before, an assistant appeared and scurried about helping me get ready for the celebration. She kept the makeup to a minimum and added hair strands to make my hair fuller and longer, falling to my shoulders in soft waves. I never had long flowing hair in my human life, so it startled and amazed me.

Once I was fully dressed, my assistant pulled out an exquisite long, gold, flowing sash that looked to be woven of gold thread. It was softer and more flexible than I expected. My assistant put it on my right shoulder this time and fastened it together at the waist under my left arm with the gold lotus pin. The sash flowed all the way down to meet the bottom of my dress. It looked stunning against the black gown.

The dress had a high neckline so no jewelry was needed. The sleeves were elbow length, which made it quite comfortable. Then my assistant brought me the opera length, spun gold gloves and placed one on each hand. The gloves reached slightly above the elbows, so no skin was available to be touched.

Thoth called out, "Are you ready? We must go." He was waiting for me near the exit door of the vehicle. To my surprise, he was still wearing his headdress, but was also immaculately dressed in his version of a black tuxedo and tails. This was obviously a very formal event. He did not have a sash this time, but he wore what appeared to be military type pins and braids, mostly in gold, on his right shoulder and draped across his chest. His formal jacket had gold piping on the lapels and down the front of the jacket as well as down the tails in the back. He also had a gold cummerbund, gold buttons, and a crisp gold bowtie, all made from the same material as my sash.

He spoke, "I have one small surprise for you before we depart." He slowly slid his hand out of an inner pocket of his jacket and revealed a magnificent, gold, Egyptian style collar necklace and placed it around my neck. It shimmered against the black dress. He continued, "This planet is known for its vast amounts of precious gold. This piece is befitting of my queen for the evening. May it be worn with joy and memories of all the good in your life."

I was overwhelmed and couldn't control the tears trickling down my cheeks. His gesture was not only thoughtful and honored the planet and people we were visiting, but it also deeply touched my heart as his faithful servant in ancient times as well as his colleague in this lifetime.

"Enough with the tears," he said gently. "We must go. It is rude and unprecedented for the guests of honor to keep the Leadership waiting. Oh, one last thing," as he motioned to my assistant to bring him something. "You need a crown befitting of the queen you are." He then reached up and placed a rather large gold crown on my head.

We traveled a few minutes, during which time I sought to compose myself. "You are wearing gloves of gold tonight not only because they look beautiful, but also they will protect you," advised Thoth. "You will need to shake many hands and I don't want you to become contaminated by local germs, nor do we want to contaminate them. Do not take your gloves off, even to eat. And when we eat, it is our food we will eat, as our systems cannot digest their food.

"When we step out, you will find the atmosphere quite heavy, making it harder to breathe. But during our travel time on the transport, your body has been prepared for that. You will also notice that it is much darker than it seems. They are farther from their sun than we are on planet Earth so they always have less light. That is why they have much larger eyes and why their skin tone is more of an ashen gray.

"Protocol here will have each guest great us with a slight bow or curtsey and a kiss on the hand. Do not lean in for a kiss on the cheek but rather offer your hand. Protection of both our eco system and our health, as well as their eco system and health, are essential to prevent any contamination. You look beautiful and are glowing; they will want to touch you.

"Once we are seated with their dignitaries in the center of the room on a slowly rotating platform, we fill be formally introduced as high-ranking guests of the planet and galaxy. They will introduce me as the Most High God of Wisdom and Knowledge and Guardian of the Universe, His Eminence Thoth. I will stand up and wave and then a few seconds later you will be introduced as my queen Fortuna. You will rise, take my hand, and we will slightly wave to the attendees as we rotate a full circle on the platform. Then we will sit, listen to several speeches, and be served our meal.

"Protocol and decorum are very important on this planet. They will keep a watchful eye on us and will delight in your charm. If we are asked to do anything you do not understand, I'll explain silently. Then just follow my lead."

We arrived at our destination and everything was as Thoth explained. The air was heavy with gravity that seemed to push down on me. There was a bit of an offensive pungent smell in the air and the light was definitely more gray than clear.

And yes, the entrance to the Chamber of Leadership and the halls were lined with their inhabitants reaching out to touch us while cheering incomprehensible or mysterious words. There were no rope lines to keep them from stepping in our path, but Thoth's energy field and presence forced them to step back as we approached.

The building was magnificent but absent of granite and marble on the floors and walls. Instead, they appeared to be of handmade construction materials and adorned with many paintings paying tribute to their hard-working inhabitants and their children.

As we entered their Celebration Hall, a giant roar of appreciation for our presence erupted. A receiving line formed and we were greeted and welcomed by what seemed like thousands of guests, all wanting to touch me, my clothing, and my gloved hands. Thoth was right. They definitely wanted to touch me.

Then we were escorted to our table in the center of the room and seated with great fanfare, music, and more cheering. When their Leadership spoke, the room went silent immediately, which surprised me. I was even more surprised when I started receiving a translated version of his words in my head. I never ceased to be amazed at Thoth's abilities. He was so far advanced beyond human technology. His abilities, even the most difficult like the instant translation of our host's message of introduction into our language in my head, was almost beyond comprehension. Thoth looked at me and winked. The crowd noticed as a hushed "awe" swept around the room.

Thoth was formally introduced, and the crowd went wild again as he stood. I was introduced after the cheering went down a couple of decibels. Thoth offered me his hand as I stood beside him and gently waved. The crowd outrageously roared again. Who couldn't love these beings? It was quite an experience.

"Their gracious and warm welcome tonight will pave the way for our ongoing meetings tomorrow," Thoth explained as we headed back to our transport vehicle. We didn't speak much as it was an overwhelming jubilant event.

I was still wearing the crown and he his headdress as we entered the privacy of our transport. He slowly removed his headdress and then gently lifted the crown off my head. "You were a queen of grace and perfection tonight. Thank you," were Thoth's final words as I quietly retreated to my dressing chamber to prepare for sleep.

A City Tour

Thoth awoke at sunrise and left to continue his meeting with the Galaxy Leadership. I, on the other hand, arose slowly. Actually, I had no idea if it was morning or evening. I was unable to relate their time to either the Library time or my human life.

I heard Thoth's voice in my head say, "It's time to arise and eat. You may also wish to do some walking on the track path in the Activities Center so your muscles do not weaken. This is a very long space distance from our home with little opportunity to move about. I will be back this afternoon. We will take a brief tour of the area and then share an early dinner on the veranda of the Presiding Leader's residence."

I brought up all the screens in the main cabin and saw Thoth in his meeting with the Galaxy Leadership. He somehow knew I had tuned in, as he looked directly at the camera for a moment and nodded.

I enjoyed my food and drink, moved to the Activities Center, and walked for quite some time while switching cameras to observe the activities of the local inhabitants as well as Thoth. Just as I was about to dress for the late afternoon activities, I noticed some tension in Thoth's body as he spoke with the Presiding Leader. It felt like something wasn't going well. The tension remained for several minutes. Then, whatever they were discussing must have resolved, because the tension quickly disappeared. Thoth rose, touched his heart with his right hand, and then bid them goodbye.

At that moment, my assistant re-appeared and readied my clothes for the outing. I wore the same neutral colored linen clothing that I wore the evening we dined under the stars in the park, only this time she placed the blue sash on my right shoulder and connected it under my left arm with the gold lotus flower broach. She placed an additional gold bar on the sash on my right shoulder to keep the sash secured. I noticed that the bar was sculpted with two ibis facing each other, faces touching. It was lovely.

I stepped out into the main cabin and Thoth, dressed similarly but with the added pins of rank, was waiting for me so we could leave. "You need one more thing," he said. He reached into his jacket and pulled out a gold tiara, a smaller version of the crown. It featured dangling nuggets of gold hanging in the lace design of the gold. He continued, "My queen must be properly dressed for our adventure."

We left and stepped into another oversized version of the Jetsons aero car. The clear bubble on the top was much larger, allowing us to stand, and it was well lit so others could see in, but we could not easily see out.

It turned out that our tour was not for us to see the area, but for the area inhabitants to see us. We travelled up and down streets, boulevards, and outlying roads and waved to jubilant adoring crowds. It was evident that they loved and treasured Thoth. Considering the magnitude of his responsibility in the universe, I was pleased to see how much they loved him.

As we neared the end of our tour, I realized there were no obvious police or military present to protect and guard such a highly regarded dignitary, an official representative of the universe, and the Creator, First Source.

Thoth internally interrupted my thought process, speaking through brain waves, "Such protection is not needed in this galaxy. Their Leadership prohibits the use of any type of force to monitor and rule over crowds. At birth, children are taught self-control, respect for self and others, equality, and truth. As they grow older and are directly connected to their Creator, they learn wisdom, the 'how to' of living in balance, peace, and harmony. Finally, they learn love of self and others, the planet, and universe. When a planet chooses to live by these rules, hope, peace, and joy abound.

"No military is necessary to prevent up-risings or maintain crowd control. They have a military, but it is more for cyber protection of the planet and the galaxy and to prevent invasions.

"We have arrived. The Presiding Leadership awaits us. There are no large crowds here, just the leaders from each inhabited planet within the galaxy. You will sit beside me just as before and will be announced after I'm presented. Put your beautiful blue opera gloves on for protection. This will be a joyful experience. You are loved here."

The Veranda Dinner and the Children

Everyone welcomed us at the Leadership's Residence with bows, curtsies, handshakes, or hand kisses. A few of the male inhabitants tried to move in and kiss my cheek, but thanks to Thoth preparing me, I was gracefully able to manage a hand kiss instead. I was grateful that the veranda had purified air and some added natural light so I could breathe and see better. Then again, maybe I had just acclimated to the atmosphere, light, and sounds.

The oversized veranda overlooked what appeared to be a children's play area. I expected the view to be that of a lake or a quiet pastoral scene, not a playground. Thoth interrupted using brain wave thought, "This planet and the galaxy is very family-oriented, so their children travel everywhere with them. What you see are the children and grandchildren of the dignitaries up here with us. Every member of each family participates in every decision and activity.

"The common thread running through each family is truth, respect, and equality always tempered with love and the highest good for all and self while bringing harm to none. It is beautiful to behold.

"When we are invited to sit and eat, the children will also be invited to their own meal in a party room below us."

I asked Thoth if it was possible to say a brief hello to the children before we left. They looked so filled with joy.

Thoth spoke to the Presiding Leader about his Queen's request. A huge smile instantly appeared on the Leader's face. A simple nod by Thoth told me my request was well received and granted.

We socialized a bit more and then were shown to our tables. This was the first time I felt some concern as I was being separated from Thoth and shown to a seat at one of the female inhabitants' tables. Thoth quickly came to my rescue and guided me to sit next to him. He was very protective of me and my wellbeing. Everyone responded with a smile as they observed his kindness and concern.

We sat promptly and immediately the Presiding Leader spoke, re-introducing Thoth and his Queen, toasted our presence, and noted Thoth's immense value to the harmony and balance in the universe. The group cheered and applauded. There must have been some type of live feed the children were watching below, as they too were cheering.

The meal arrived. We ate, shared pleasantries, and drank. The meal ended as promptly as it began. The Presiding Leader stood, made a farewell toast, and we exchanged farewell wishes to each guest in the receiving line.

Then came the fun! We made our way to the children's lower veranda area. I didn't need an interpreter to understand their joy and happiness at seeing us. They immediately formed a single line, with the littlest ones being held by older siblings. I saw the joy in their sparkling eyes. One by one they each bowed and curtsied with massive grins on their unusually beautiful faces. They glowed like lightening bugs in the early evening light of a meadow on an early summer day on Earth.

Thoth smiled as he recognized how much the children and I were enjoying this moment. The children reacted to his smile with giggles of joy. I thought to myself, "These inhabitants are so observant and respond approvingly to even to the smallest acknowledgement of kindness or appreciation."

By the time we returned to the security of our transport vehicle, I was exhausted. It turned out to be an eventful and long day, but it was wonderful and hugely successful for Thoth. The joy of sharing our love and kindness with these beings filled my heart with joy.

Thoth spoke as he removed his headdress and my tiara, "Our work here is done a day early. We will depart in three hours and thirty-three minutes. That will provide us the exact timing we need to reach our resting space in the transit route to home.

"The Presiding Leadership and the inhabitants loved you. That helped greatly in our talks. We were able to resolve the external issues facing the entire galaxy during our meetings. Our pictures with the children are being broadcast throughout the galaxy, and you are being declared the Queen of compassion, love, and joy.

Enroute to Home

The next day. I slept through the entire first third of our trip, which took place in silence and darkness. As much as I would have enjoyed seeing the starlit galaxy, we traveled so fast that all I saw were streaking light lines and darkness. It was distracting and hypnotic for some — nauseating for others. The viewing canopy was closed during travel time with a view of the universe showing in slow motion. It didn't matter. I fell into a deep prolonged sleep.

We reached the point in our return home where we needed to stay stationary for a period of time and wait for the timing of planetary alignments in the universe for safe passage and the landing window in the Library's time zone.

There was no landing or refueling station. We simply occupied space in a specific dark area of the universe until the universe was ready for us to continue. It felt like we were floating on an air cushion, which would catapult us forward at a moment's notice.

We always sat in our unique space travel chairs for departure and arrival, although the movement was barely noticeable. The vehicle certainly used technologies far from humanity's discovery.

"Are you awake?" Thoth asked quietly. "Food and drink are waiting for you."

I dashed to my Dressing Chamber, prepared for my day of travel, and joined Thoth at the table.

"You had quite an experience being my Queen during our visit," Thoth said as he gleefully showed me his transparent universe download screen. "Look. There is a picture of His Eminence and his Queen spending time with the children. Just before we left last night a messenger arrived from the Presiding Leadership with a small gift for each of us. Open it," he said as he nodded toward the box on the table.

I looked down at the table and saw a gold foil-wrapped box with a small tag that simply said, "Queen Fortuna." I carefully picked it up, I noticed that the box had some weight, I painstakingly unwrapped the gold foil, understanding its monetary value. Inside was a royal blue box that matched the color or our sashes at the veranda reception.

My eyes grew wide and incredulous as I opened the box and saw an oversized gold ring beautifully sculpted with a lotus flower blossom. Unable to contain my joy, I spoke out loud, "Oh my goodness! It is exquisite. It is similar to the pin on my sash."

Thoth replied, "They wished to thank you for your gracious kindness and joy you brought to their planet and galaxy. Their wish for you is eternal good health, success, and joy. They hoped you will use is as your seal and wear it often.

"I received one as well with an ibis sculpted on mine. It is very handsome! It is the small kindnesses and pleasant courtesies that win other's hearts and minds, not physical force, laws, and intimidation."

Conversation flowed as we ate and drank. Sometimes we sat in silence. I often found myself almost in a trance as I picked his brain about the esoteric, ancient Egypt, and the Medieval Times. At one point, perhaps a bit unamused by all my questions, he reminded me that I could access all that information from the Library even when in outer space.

I smiled. He knew I would rather hear the answers directly from him. His voice drew me in as he brought each story to life. The last few questions I chose to ask at that moment were about each galaxy. "Are they all similar with a central sun? Do they all have planetary cycles like astrological cycles similar to the stars in our sky? Do they have cycles that are like a roadmap of the past, present, and future?

He responded, "Every galaxy has millions of stars of varying sizes, numerous planets, and up to seven suns. Revolving around each sun you will usually find several planets of varying sizes. Each of these sun clusters or solar systems are filled with exact movement, distance, and various energy fields that keep them in place, preventing catastrophic disasters.

"Some of these solar systems within a galaxy have lifeforms; others do not. Many lifeforms exist and do not necessarily look human. Some are in their infancy stages like Galaxy 7; others are far superior to humans and our solar system.

"As to astrology, every solar system has its own roadmap written in the stars, what you call astrology or the houses in the sky. That roadmap, if correctly interpreted, can reveal the past, explain the present, and predict the future, just as on planet Earth.

"It is unfortunate that astrology was pushed aside on Earth during the Middle Ages. There is much wisdom and knowledge to be found by studying the movement and relationships of the stars, and their importance to the planet, events, and individuals. Astrology was the only scientific tool used by the Atlanteans and the ancients. So, the answer is yes. Every solar system has a roadmap built into the stars."

The Return Home

We returned to our travel seats in preparation for our take off to home. The canopy was closed and the seats reclined into our makeshift beds. I neither heard nor saw anything as I fell fast asleep.

I woke with a start hearing Thoth say, "Wake up! You must see this. We are approaching Earth and you can see a meteor shower off to the left. It is spectacular, as is the night sky."

I sat up the moment he said meteor shower. It was beautiful, almost like a massive firework's display high in the night sky. I was sure we were close enough to Earth that humans could observe it if awake.

I stared out the windows for a long time, enjoying the view. Thoth said, "We must prepare for arrival. Everything needs to be readied for landing, including our chairs."

It was hard to take my eyes away from the night sky and its meteor extravaganza. But I had to tend to my duties before landing.

Finally, Thoth announced, "We are home, back at the same platform we left seven days ago." He placed his headdress on.

Much to my surprise, as the door opened, I saw a cheering crowd awaiting our arrival. I had never seen more than a handful of people at the Library Complex, except for the reunion party and the orchestra in the park experience. I questioned, "Who are all these people? Where did they come from? And why are they cheering?"

Reading my thoughts, Thoth said, "They are all the wonderful residents and employees of the Abode and the Library of Wisdom and Knowledge. They are welcoming us home from our long journey to Galaxy 6 and our safe return. They are reveling in our success, especially that of Thoth's Queen Fortuna. They now understand your importance and recognize the vast influence you will have on others."

I blushed and turned back to thank my dressing assistant for all her help. "Namaste," I said to her just before leaving the vehicle. She brought her hands together, nodded, and said, "Namaste" in return. The crowd cheered even louder.

Thoth said, "We must go. Our transport awaits us. We need to go through a purification process before we can re-enter the main complex to make sure we have not carried back any hitchhikers or unknown contaminants. Each of our garments, jewelry, and personal belongings will be similarly processed before their safe return to our chambers.

"Hurry. Let's go. Food and drink await us," he said as we waved goodbye to our welcoming crowd.

A few hours later, feeling somewhat refreshed, I went into the Main Hall where Thoth was already seated and reviewing the downloads from the various galaxies. He said, "You've made headlines in every galaxy. Our visit to Galaxy 6 is the lead story in every galaxy across the universe."

After some fear and trepidation, I finally got up the courage to speak and told Thoth, "I am concerned about those headlines. First, it is you, Thoth, who should be the center of attention. The lead story should be about the success of your meetings, not me. Second, I'm not really a queen, Thoth's Queen, or any form of royalty."

Thoth seemed surprised and taken aback by my comments. He assumed I would appreciate the adoration and the honor of being called his Queen. He went silent for several minutes, which was highly unusual for him. He always had an instant response or comeback to any verbal question or thoughts I had.

I found his silence deafening and extremely unsettling. I even questioned myself as to whether I should have spoken out. Perhaps this time I really did speak out of turn.

Thoth, who was always very attentive to my slightest reaction, finally broke the uneasy silence. "I'm sorry," he said, "We are definitely not in the teacher/student relationship we had in Ancient Egypt. I made many assumptions in my actions and decisions on our trip. Please accept my apologies. We are colleagues now with a Creator-centric unified intent of bringing hope, peace, and joy to planet Earth by re-connecting the masses to their Creator. In our current relationship we are one with each other and one with the One.

"I should have consulted with you first about my plans for this trip. I assumed you would enjoy playing the role of Queen. Actually, I even assumed that you would want to take this trip versus staying here alone and spending time in the Library. You know how I take great pleasure in surprising you with things that I know will bring you joy, such as the music in the bandstand at the park. For all of this I am deeply sorry and will endeavor to maintain our equal colleague relationship.

"However, you must know how much I respect you, your strengths, and your desire to share the Creator's words and love with the masses. You are my Queen here in the Library and whenever we travel together."

Thoth waited quietly and hopefully for me to respond.

After collecting my thoughts and taking several deep breaths, I looked him straight in the eyes and spoke out loud. "Thoth, I have had great respect and admiration for you ever since our first lifetime together as your scribe. You treated me with dignity, honesty, and compassion in a world where little of any of those existed. Throughout lifetimes I've remembered your teachings, wisdom, and my admiration of you. You truly represent wisdom, knowledge, and judgment, using them appropriately to improve self and others while bringing no harm to anyone.

"Therefore, I was surprised at the set of circumstances during our visit to the Presiding Leadership on Galaxy 6. It seemed like my participation in the events, while being most enjoyable and touching my heart with joy, were a bit less than truthful.

"With that said, I accept your apology, as your intent was in the best interest of the many, giving hope, peace, and joy to all while bringing harm to no one except perhaps my ego. I appreciate all I know of you from our previous lifetime together and honor you for who you are, your wisdom, knowledge, and the role you play in creating heaven on Earth and in the universe.

"And, it is an honor to be thought of as your Queen."

Thoth let out a huge sigh of relief and allowed a broad smile to overtake his face. He spoke, "Today you are the master of wisdom and knowledge and I, the student, have learned. Thank you.

"Shall we eat?"

Rebalancing

Later that same day, Thoth asked if I would like to go to the park. I loved the park and was about to eagerly accept the invitation when I chose to hesitate for a second. I thought, "He heard me earlier and has asked me to go. He did not assume I would go or tell me to go." Thoth immediately smiled, realizing I got the message. I appreciated the ask instead of the assumption and answered a definite yes.

Off we went. Thoth insisted we use our hover platform instead of walk. I could tell he was still a bit concerned about my wellbeing and did not want me to needlessly stress my healing energy field, especially after such a long and energy demanding trip.

"The float awaits us," Thoth said as we arrived by the lake in the park. "It is important to rebalance a human body after stressful events, such as our trip to Galaxy 6.

Stress in a very short time period can reduce your immune system and significantly drain your energy if not brought back into balance and alignment regularly. Let's go and take a leisurely walk in the labyrinth. It will bring us balance, quiet our hearts and minds, and bring our physical, spiritual, and mental sides into alignment.

"You, we, have much work ahead in your human life. I don't want your wellbeing to take a nose dive and your goals and objectives to go out of alignment because of stress, including some of my unintended and unacceptable actions and assumptions."

I smiled and nodded in acknowledgement and acceptance. We walked in silence with our energy fields united in the cause ahead of us. We lingered in the middle of the labyrinth, both in deep thought and communicating with our Creator, removing any lingering stress, harmful backstories, and negativity. I felt both of our energy fields refill with light, love, peace, and joy. Thoth acknowledged feeling the same as we embraced the moment in the sunshine.

We continued the remainder of our labyrinth walk, which reversed every turn we made when we entered. That is how the balancing takes place within and physically. Whether on the way into the labyrinth or on the way out, you experience as many left turns as right turns for complete balance.

Unlike a maze, a labyrinth has no walls, only the foot path, and there are no dead ends. The path will automatically lead you to the center, the most spiritual area, and then you retrace the path to exit.

"Well done," Thoth said as we emerged later. "Would you like a peaceful place to rest and eat? I know the perfect spot. The water vehicle awaits our return."

We floated around the lake and enjoyed the colors and the birds singing. After a short time, we debarked at the footpath that led to the gazebo where food and drink awaited us. It must have been late afternoon as the roses were particularly fragrant. I also noticed that the seating arrangement had changed. No longer were the chairs seated at a 45 degree angle but rather they faced each other so eye-to-eye conversation could take place and equality and respect are in balance.

As we sat Thoth spoke, "The human was never designed by the Creator to deal with the volume of stress that attacks it daily. That came from tampering by controlling civilizations after we left Ancient Egypt. Then followed greed, control, and servitude. Each of which piled their own forms of stress onto the human.

"In the 21st century, it has reached the tipping point for humanity. Every stressor from early millennia is still affecting humanity, with greed and control heaped on top. The level of stress has exponentially increased with the addition of mega political factions trying to take over the world and the incessant intrusion of technology. Humanity has no escape route unless they adopt a lifestyle that includes stress relaxing measures.

"Parks should have labyrinths, even if it is only a footpath marked by stones. Corporations should build stress relieving labyrinths within their walls and in outdoor spaces where weather permits. Large family neighborhoods should include labyrinths in the original plan of the development.

"If these kinds of steps are not taken, natural immunity levels will continue to decline and humanity will morph into a disease-prone, Godless, chaos-filled abyss.

"Humanity must act now and reverse this massive invisible trend."

> "The human was never designed by the Creator to deal with the volume of stress that attacks it daily. Humanity has no escape route unless they adopt a lifestyle that includes stress relaxing measures."

Family Focused

The next day I awakened early thanks to Crystal. She had just discovered our return and was full of energy. She bounded up on my bed, so excited that she couldn't stop wiggling. Her tail and head were trying to go in two different directions at the same time.

Thoth laughed out loud in the Great Room, as he knew what I was experiencing. He experienced the same welcome when he picked her up in the Unconditional Joy Chamber where my lifetimes of loved animals and birds dwelled. Crystal loved it there. She made many friends, all of them loving her mom.

Finally, she and I joined Thoth at the table. He was reviewing his Galaxy downloads and asked he if could show me something. I appreciated the ask, knowing this could have been a touchy subject. There were dozens more pictures of our visit to Galaxy 6. Some featured Thoth only, calling him The Most High Eminence, and gave him accolades for the successful meetings. Others showed us at the banquet while standing and waving to the attendees. But the majority showed our visit to the children and how that brought joy to every child and parent there. More important, it gave joy and encouragement to every child that saw the pictures around the universe.

Thoth explained, "Galaxy 6 happens to be very focused on the family as a core for their way of living and leadership. Children on other planets are not so fortunate, as is the case in our galaxy and our planet.

"Children are violated, taken advantage of, and abused on planet Earth, and only the few are rescued.

"Those pictures and your attendance at the events have offered hope to millions of children in the universe that a better day is coming for all of them."

As I held Crystal, my heart ached for all the children of the world. It did not matter whether they looked like human children, had large eyes, or gray skin. I wanted to hug them all and do whatever I could to give them a better life.

"You can," interjected Thoth. "That is one of the objectives of your book *Looking Within*. When people reconnect with their Creator, God, First Source, they will learn truth and be given a new perspective on how children and others should be treated.

"Prejudice and hate need to be banished forever from Earth. This one truth will make waves and reach into the corners of every Galaxy. Children will finally be free and treated like equals in the family unit. And then the family unit as a whole can start to return communities back into the original intent of the Creator.

"A community should be filled with compassion, respect, equality, love, and joy. This is why it was so important for you to join me on our trip into the universe. Your presence glowed and reached out to touch every child's heart whether there or in other galaxies far away or in our own.

"Thank you for who you are and what you've accomplished."

The Exceptional Spiritual Chamber

"We are heading to a new Chamber today—one you will not have thought of as having spiritual significance," Thoth explained as we headed down another corridor.

"So many books have been written about me emphasizing alchemy and the philosopher's stone when instead they should have focused on the humanity aspect of the alchemy—the human heart. It's the life-giving force of Creation, the moment when that first beat of the heart appears.

"Humanity questions when life begins. It begins long before most understand. The moment the heart beats for the first time is when a child's life begins. At that point, there is no body so to speak, and there is no brain, at least not the brain we think of as a human brain.

"The heart comes with its own version of a built-in brain that immediately starts putting the millions of steps in place necessary to grow the human body, organs, bone structure, muscles, eyes, and lungs to name a few components. The heart is a finely-tuned data processing system. It controls things from that first heart beat to birth since the fetal brain doesn't begin to form until at least the third week of gestation. It is the heart that is in control.

"It is the heart that receives and maintains the connection with the Creator, not the brain. The Creator communicates through the heart, not the brain or the ego. It is the brain, the ego part of humans, that disconnects from their Creator and starts to build walls instead of leaving that connection open to allow a free-flowing two-way dialogue with God."

By now we had walked a great distance. A door opened and we walked into a purification chamber and then into the Healing Chamber. I was confused. We had been here a few times before.

Thoth corrected me and said, "Follow me. Yes, we've been in this section of the Chamber but not the smaller one on the far side of the room. To get into that space we need to pass through another smaller purification room."

As we passed through the purification room, the next set of doors opened. All I saw were transparent baskets after baskets filled with babies. They were wonderful little babies. Some were asleep, a few were fussing, and a couple were screaming, testing out their vocal cords.

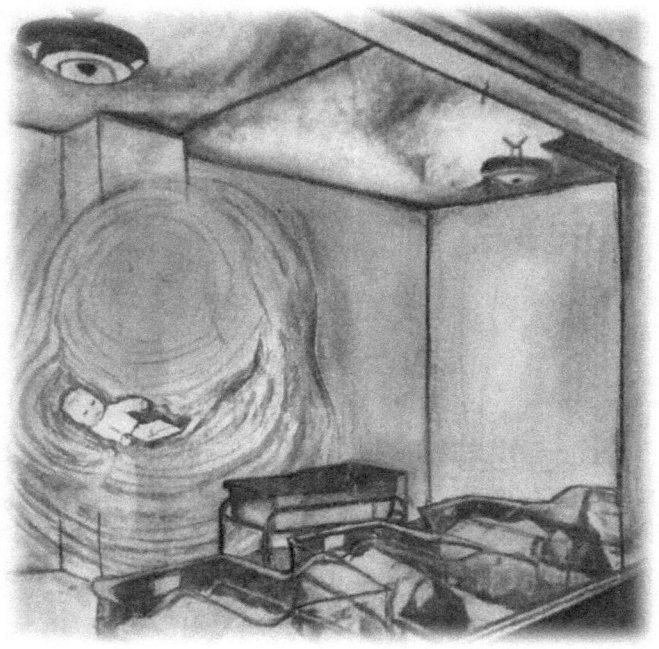

Thoth noted the wide smile on my face and continued, "This is the most spiritual area in the whole Library Complex. This is where human life begins. Their lives began with their first heart beat but this is where their physical life begins. When their heart is programmed properly and receives the proper nurturing and nourishing, love, and care, God's last touch is that of breath as they enter the physical world.

"At the moment of physical birth, a child fully knows the true love and connection of the Creator energy source. That child is magical, beautiful, a treasure to hold and behold.

"If you want to see your Creator, look into the eyes of a newborn child; the Creator resides there. That physical birth is proof of the Creator's existence. They are a vision to behold and respect. They come with a deep spiritual connection that is often almost immediately broken by parents and family members. Parent's need to reconnect to their Creator now so they can support and encourage their babies to stay connected. That is the greatest gift a parent can give a baby."

> "If you want to see your Creator, look into the eyes of a newborn child; the Creator resides there."

Responsible for Self

"As you can see," Thoth continued, "life moves on daily in the Library of Wisdom and Knowledge as above in the human world. However here, there are no forced expectations by others for your performance or productivity as the babies grow into productive prosperous adults. This self-responsibility concept removes a great deal of stress. It also puts each baby/child/person in control of self and their future. Self-responsibility is held in the highest regard here.

"Once a person as an adult agrees to do a task, they and only they are responsible for doing and completing that task, whether it's in the area of food production or transport vehicle maintenance.

"No one looks over their shoulder prodding them, disparaging them, or for that matter encouraging them. There is someone always nearby should they seek help or require additional information or encouragement. But the completion of their task is solely their responsibility.

"When one commits to a task, that person has the complete understanding of the importance of the task, how it fits into the grand scheme of things, and how it is relevant to the over-arching project. For example, if someone in the food production area chooses to skip overlooking the life-giving watering system for two days and doesn't find the break in the water lines that needed instant repair two days earlier, hundreds of people could starve from lack of food due to the plants dying from lack of water.

"In the case of the transport vehicle maintenance person, lack of proper attention and maintenance to a vehicle could cause a mishap, death, or leave people endlessly lost in space until another transport can be re-routed to rescue them. That doesn't even take into consideration the need, time, and expense of a rescue crew to help the stranded passengers, meet their unexpected needs, and repair the transport vehicle so it could return home safely.

"Every job is important and when performed properly will be rewarded. This work ethic and philosophy is implanted at birth, again at a very early age in a child, and is constantly reinforced by the parents.

"It is the family unit that is at the foundation of every successful future adult and work contributor. By the time a child enters school these values are well instilled in the child's heart and life ethic. It is thought of as their contribution to society or for living on planet Earth, giving something back to the world and honoring their Creator."

In order to get Thoth to stop and take a breath, I mentally drew a picture of a soapbox with a person standing on it. Thoth caught the soapbox graphic; he stopped talking and took several very long deep breaths. I encouraged him to go on but not until we ate and drank so his body, mind, and spirt could provide him balance within.

While very passionate about this topic, he did appreciate my genuine concern, so he paused and slowly partook in the nourishment on the table. Simultaneously,

Crystal bounded into the room and right up into his lap. They both rejoiced to be in each other's company again. We all then sat quietly enjoying the energetic presence of each other's company and the fluffy joy Crystal brought to each of us.

Thoth continued, "The family unit is the basis for creating such a firm foundation. When a man and woman unite in a lifetime relationship, it is done in honor of the Creator's love and commitment to ensure humanity continues.

"As equal partners in the relationship, they choose what and how each role they will be responsible for in the relationship, commit to sharing time with each other, as well as time to communicate with their Creator, First Source or God. These conversations are not limited to one and done but are on-going throughout their lives. As they embark on growing their family size, they will expand their conversations including their older children to discuss the new responsibilities and commitments.

"How do they know to do this? They were taught verbally and through example by their parents. If they didn't learn it there, other family members, friends, and neighbors ban together as a support system to help them. Therefore, the quality of family life becomes the quality of the community they live in, and the future of their children. Each and every child has the right to choose the life they wish to pursue while growing up. But the overwhelming majority choose the life they see displayed every day by their loving family.

"Once a child reaches school age, they are ready to socialize appropriately and interact with others. Their importance as a person and the role they choose in life is highly re-enforced at every level in their school experience. The closer a child gets to the continuing education or job training decision, the more they are taught about their importance as a person, how to choose a job or a career path best suited for them, and what role they will play in the long-term vision of that career path. Additionally, they will learn the performance impact their job will have on the overall functioning of that project or end outcome.

"Families are the basis for and the most import foundational tool for creating happy, balanced, productive adults that honor the Creator and guarantee future civilization will be filled with hope, peace, and joy."

Community Park

"I'm going on a field trip today. Would you like to join me?" asked Thoth as we finished eating. Crystal jumped to her feet and excitedly wagged her tail. She ran to Thoth and looked up hopefully at him as if to say, "Me, me, me. I want to go." He acknowledged her excitement and reassured her that she could join us if her mom allowed it.

Even though I didn't show quite the same excitement Crystal did, I always loved Thoth's adventures. I appreciated him asking and nodded my head yes.

As we prepared to leave, Thoth put his headdress on. He then placed a container filled with ice, food, and beverages on our transport vehicle. The three of us boarded the vehicle. Crystal stood between us and was safely belted to the vehicle; her hair, ears, and tail were flying backwards like a dog on point as we sped down and up the corridors. I questioned if we were headed to a picnic but Thoth refused to respond.

We moved along quickly up to the cross corridor, turned a sharp right, and then proceeded forward again. A new doorway revealed itself, opened, and closed behind us.

We arrived in a small city or village with a large square park in front of us. It was alive with families and children playing games like tag, soccer, tennis, and volleyball. Joy, fun, and laughter abounded. A large portion of the park was covered by the canopy of a massive tree. It reminded me of the town square in Lahaina, Maui, one of the Hawaiian Islands where, prior to the devastating fire of 2023, an enormous banyan tree with all its offshoots covered the entire city block of its Center Square Park.

This park was beautiful, magical, and rang out with joy.

The three of us headed towards some park tables under the tree where we could sit and observe the park with its many occupants.

Thoth explained, "Parks like this are required everywhere throughout our system. It is important that families play together and get outdoors to breathe fresh air and be in the sunshine. Plus, they always include a labyrinth for personal quiet space.

"Playing together develops better family relationships, being outdoors promotes better health, and being active promotes stronger bodies.

"You will notice there are no electronic devices out here; they're not allowed. There is no advertising on billboards or big screens to distract from the togetherness and joy everyone experiences. Occasionally, if there is a spirited event, competition games, playoffs, or news, a big screen will pop up in different places around the park so those using the park can see and hear what is happening while being together as a family unit. Otherwise, the park is a technology-free zone."

By now, people started to notice our presence. I imagined it would be difficult to not notice an important dignitary like Thoth with his ibis headdress. Many people waved, but only a few came to our table to interact with Thoth. He carefully introduced me as his colleague and her companion Crystal. Crystal, of course, loved all the attention, and I noticed that she was much better behaved when Thoth was nearby than with just me. Thoth winked at me in appreciation for the compliment while never saying a word.

After eating and enjoying the shade of the tree, Thoth spoke, "Huge emphasis is placed on the family unit. This is how children learn respect for the older generations and how to nurture and care for others. They learn how to negotiate disputes so each side can win on the basis of right and wrong, as well as the rules of respect, honor, all and equality. They also learn self-control and self-responsibility as they interact with their extended family members along with other families. They even learn how to strike up conversations with potential girlfriends or boyfriends in a safe setting. Ultimately, all these life lessons are providing them wisdom when introduced in the presence of love.

"The children respond the same way to their parents. No, it hasn't always been this way, but slowly through deliberate intent and thought we have shifted to a family-centric society. The parents are equal co-partners and participate as equals in the responsibility of ensuring that the family is strong and has solid participation in the 'family first' thought process. You can observe it in action as we sit here in the park."

The day flew by quickly. Crystal was tired and tried to nap as we prepared for our return home.

Honest Interactions and a Deep Spiritual Experience

"Yes, here it is." I heard Thoth say. I couldn't discern if he was talking to himself or to Crystal, as she was gone from my bed. Thoth continued, "Did you take my sandals to play with as a chew toy?"

Upon hearing that, I jumped up, grabbed a robe, wrapped it around me quickly, and raced into the Main Hall to see what Crystal destroyed. Expecting to see a disaster, I instead saw Thoth sitting on the floor playing with Crystal while rescuing his sandal, which appeared to be unharmed.

I must have had a ghastly look on my face and looked disheveled from arising so quickly. Thoth looked up and with a grin on his face said, "You look lovely my Queen." In total embarrassment, I quickly returned to my sleeping chamber and properly prepared for my day.

Upon my return to the Great Hall, food and drink awaited me along with Thoth and Crystal in his lap. I hadn't seen this side of Crystal before. The loving energy in the Abode was nurturing for her as well. In fact, I had never seen the more personable, softer, and humorous side of Thoth before either. The hieroglyphic images of him chiseled or painted on Ancient Egyptian tombs always portrayed him as someone very serious and perhaps to be avoided at all costs.

Thoth was engaged in reviewing his galaxy download and flipping through the screen quickly as if looking for something. I never asked about his work unless he wished to share. I knew he would tell me if there was something happening of interest to me. I respected his privacy and didn't want him to think I was prying.

He immediately interrupted my thought saying, "There is a major difference between someone prying and someone showing interest! I would be happy to share more information with you if appropriate, but I won't share it if I feel you are not interested. After all, I can't read your mind." He then burst into a huge smile.

"Oh, I'm sorry, Thoth," I replied. "I made a bad assumption. I am always interested in what you do. Your knowledge and responsibilities are so vast that I could listen to you and your stories without ceasing. My quietness is out of respect for your privacy. I will ask more often, but now that you know I am always interested, perhaps you could share more as well."

"You have become a very wise Queen," Thoth spoke deliberately. "Your wisdom serves you well and will equally serve millions.

"Now we must go. A walk on the labyrinth and lunch in the park awaits us, if you'd like to join me."

We headed to the park after dropping Crystal off in the play area with all her new best friends.

I wondered if this was a day of relaxation and regeneration or if it was a teaching day. Or perhaps it was both wrapped into one. It didn't really matter; I loved spending time in Thoth's energy field. This lifetime had all the kindness and teaching from my ancient scribe days, but this time I was experiencing the depth of this ancient god, who now called me Queen and openly shared truth, knowledge, and wisdom all wrapped somehow in an unconditional love energy field I felt at all times.

By now we were on our floating platform slowly making our way around the lake and experiencing the shared solitude, beauty, colors, and fragrances. No words. No thoughts. Just being. It was awe-inspiring, almost overwhelming with peace and joy. In fact, the entire journey, from the lake to the labyrinth, was so overwhelmingly peace and joy-filled that tears welled up in my eyes and my heart overflowed with love. Silence in this case truly was golden. Imagine just being—with no past, no future, nothing but presence and being. I had never experienced this feeling before. It was so wonderful that I wished I knew how to have everyone share it.

"Everyone can share it through you, your books, or by reaching this point of deep connection by themselves," said Thoth. "Humanity needs to experience this to become whole again. What you are feeling is the undefinable, awe-inspiring as you call it, experience of being fully immersed in the Creator's infinite love.

"Once you've experienced it, you never want to be without it. It is the true philosopher's stone. The alchemists of old, even today, think the philosophers stone is a magical or mythical substance that turns a base metal into gold. All this time has passed and they still don't get it. It is all about changing or transforming the human from a base existence into the spiritual being intended by the Creator where they can always be connected and bask in the love and glory of the Creator."

We both fell silent again as we stepped onto the labyrinth path, deep in our own thoughts and feelings. God's overwhelming personal love bathed us as we proceeded in silence, basking in the warmth of the day. I wanted everyone to share and experience this feeling, as I knew it had the power to change people's lives. This feeling was what alchemists unknowingly sought—the ultimate philosopher's stone within. The steps to get there were laid out in esoteric studies long ago. But instead of applying the steps to base metals, they need to be applied to self and transformation within.

"Well," said Thoth as he was listening to my thoughts. "Humanity continues to look without when they need to look within. The answers to the future greatness of humankind all lie within. They cannot achieve the abundant love and joy the Creator has stockpiled for each and every child of the universe without looking within and seeking transformation. You have experienced this on a very deep heart level. I could feel your heart merging with our Creator and weeping in gratitude."

> "Humanity continues to look without when they need to look within. The answers to the future greatness of humankind all lie within."

In silence again we boarded our small floating transport and glided quietly to the canal that leads to the gazebo. As usual, food and drink awaited us, as did the wonderful fragrances of the roses. We sat facing each other, talking quietly and thoroughly enjoying the warm afterglow of such an almost indescribable experience of our Creator's love.

We remained in the presence of the Creator as the sun set, revealing the first evening star. It was the most unique and exceptional relaxation and connection I have ever experienced. I have been on my spiritual journey, in some ways, all my life. This by far touched the deepest part of my being.

Planet Earth

"I'm planning a distance trip. Will you join me," asked Thoth. "You don't have to be a queen this time unless you'd like to be presented as my Queen."

I loved the intrigue and the way he invited me this time, asking not telling me. Our colleague relationship had blossomed into equality. I admired this in Thoth and respected him immensely for the god he was, his wisdom and knowledge, and the role he played in the universe. Some with his importance and position would not treat me with such equality and respect.

I looked at him and realized I hadn't answered him. He had a concerned look on his face.

"Oh, of course. Yes. I'd love to join you on this trip. It sounds wonderful. Where are we going? When do we leave? How long will be gone?'"

"We leave this afternoon at 3:33 human time. Everything is being prepared."

Thoth hurried off to look after some pressing matters that needed his attention. I spent some with Crystal who already understood the word "go" did not include her. But she did love spending time with all her new friends in the Unconditional Joy Chamber, where I took her before preparing to leave. I left knowing she would be in good company and well cared for.

I didn't know where Thoth was taking me, but I decided to bring two candles with me: the huge one with the one oversized wick and a second one with two wicks. I loved watching the double flames dance.

It was 3:00 when I met Thoth at the Great Hall door and stepped out into the corridor. We were whisked away to the distant travel area in the Transportation Chamber. Thoth wore his ibis headdress.

When we arrived, we were directed into a specified "RESTRICTED" area. We passed through to a special long transit capsule and boarded quickly. It was as if Thoth didn't want to be seen. Our belongings, food, and drink were already aboard. At exactly 3:33 the capsule left the platform and proceeded to the terminal where the power source was attached, and then our trip began. Just like the last trip to Galaxy 6, the capsule tilted to a 37 degree angle, rose straight up into the sky, and catapulted forward, unseen by the human eye or current technology.

Thoth removed his headdress and said, "I thought you would enjoy a bit of a history lesson, so we are traveling back in time. We are going back multiple millions of years ago when the land on Earth was all one mass, and we will fast forward from there so you can watch the land mass separate into what we now call continents.

"We are actually going to watch planet Earth evolve as noted on the belt of equator of the planetarium in the Galaxy Chamber. You are about to see the original and first documentary up close and personal of how the planet evolved once the Creator brought it into existence through thought.

"We have arrived in the proper age of the planet and are going to just hang out here in a safe location in the

Milky Way, close enough to see yet far enough to not get hurt.

"You can see planet Earth, the blue marble, as humans call it, directly in front of us. As it rotates, you will think it looks lopsided with so much blue water dominating the surface. At least 70% of the planet was covered in water when the land mass began to split into large sections.

"The planet is cooling. The massive amounts of rain helped that process and allowed the land mass to turn a bit green here and there with the first forms of vegetation life. As the molten iron core of the Earth continues to cool, tectonic plates will slide and bump into each other. Sometimes they will collide and create mountains pointing toward the sky, such as that mountain range we will eventually call the Alps.

"When tectonic plates spread further apart instead of colliding, great ravines form, pointing toward the western sections of the land mass. The great bursts of fire come from areas where the earth layer was not solidly formed and thick. It will be blasted open from the molten furnace below the surface, much like an incredible fireworks display."

Not only could we see the long-distance view through very powerful telescopes, but he also had equally powerful cameras aboard filming the process with high lens magnification that made it feel like the planet was only 30,000 feet below. It was like watching a high energy play or live performance.

As he fast forwarded time, we saw a major ravine of blue show up in the area known today as the western edge of northern Europe and the eastern edge of North

America. Nothing had broken away yet, but you could see it beginning. Other mountain ranges started to take form in the far east in what is now called India but the country was not quite formed yet, as that part of the land mass was still undefined by the ocean's fury.

Thoth spoke, "Watch, there it goes. It is spectacular."

I was glued to the screen and telescopes. I watched as the land ripped apart. At first it appeared as jagged lines that looked like a million little rivers clawing their way through the 20 plus miles depth of the Earth's crust. I saw constant explosions of molten lava from below the Earth's crust where the land crust was weak or thin. Some of the mountain ranges showed live volcanos belching their angry heat and lava upward to the sky. The pressures under the crust were massive and the heat broke through at the weakest points wherever we looked. In other spaces water viciously tore the land mass apart wherever it could find weakness.

It was frightening yet ever so hypnotizing and awe inspiring to watch the sheer force of energy as the result of the Creator's single thought that created our galaxy and planet.

"Finally," said Thoth. "Look at the enormous piece of land that is slowly moving west, allowing the Atlantic Ocean to form. There are small fissures breaking land off in the north. They will eventually form Iceland and Greenland.

"As that land mass travels west, there is also movement on the eastern land mass where large sections of land took shape forming the outline of India and Australia with what appears to be a land bridge from

Australia to the mainland. For quite some time Australia was much larger until millions of years later as ocean levels rose and completely covered much of the northern part in water and left only a string of islands. There are other small islands that formed the same way, such as New Zealand, Japan, and Hawaii, to name just a few.

"Watch", said Thoth as he directed my eyes to a particular area. "The last major break is about to happen. Another very large piece of land that once touched current Africa and South America is now breaking away into a rather strange rounded mass of land that looks a little like an elephant's head with its trunk pointing toward South America. In fact, for many years it remained connected by a thin land bridge until the waters rose, just as the current land bridge where Russia and North American were once connected.

"As the land cooled and started to settle into its new location, additional mountain ranges exploded up into the air due to the tectonic plate movements and trapped heat and gases exploding from below forming ranges in Alaska, the Rocky Mountains, and the Andes. In other area geysers were formed to let off steam. It's a spectacular light show, don't you think?"

We watched for many more hours as the land morphed and changed like a chameleon. It was a beautiful birthing process of this land we call home.

Thoth said, "I'm hungry and you must be exhausted. Shall we dine tonight among the stars rather than under the stars? Let's prepare for dinner."

I retreated to my dressing chamber where a fresh change of clothing awaited me. But there were two choices: one was my daily wear; the other was the clothing specially made for the time we dined under the stars in the park. I chose the latter. The dressing assistant appeared and helped me dress and do my hair. Upon completion, I was about to leave the room when she stepped in and called me back. She placed the lovely blue sash over my head and onto my right shoulder and clasped it together below the waist on the left side with the beautiful gold lotus flower broach. Next, she added the lapis blue and gold lotus necklace and the two gold band cuffs on each wrist.

We chose to sit in the main cabin so we had a 200 degree view. The canopy cover of the transport slid back to expose more of the solar system. It truly felt like we were sitting among the stars. I was grateful that Thoth didn't slide the floor back too. I don't think I could have handled seeing nothing below me expect dark empty sky and stars. My assistant must have found my candles, as the one with the two flames was already on the table and lit.

Thoth arrived at the same time dressed in the same casual formal wear from the park. He asked if I liked the view and invited me to sit and dine among the stars.

Planet Earth Part Two

We arrived back home at the Abode after the rewind of millions of years so I could have a better understanding about how the Earth formed and worked. It remained the topic of discussion on our not so lengthy warp speed journey home. He told me, "Remember, the land masses on planet Earth continue to evolve. That process never stops.

"The last major change happened when a massive meteor crashed into Earth and created a hole that is now the Caribbean Islands and the Gulf of Mexico. Not only did it alter the water levels for the planet but it also caused a planet wide blackout for years, killing the vegetation and all the animals like the dinosaurs. Then came the cold, the ice caps, and the glaciers. Up until then, all the land masses had vegetation and a warm climate. This is why the hairy mammoths and their remains with undigested tropical vegetation in the stomachs are being found in Siberia and look like they were flash frozen. That is exactly what happened. Some were flash frozen, while others instantly disintegrated from the heat.

"That impact also bought about the polar ice caps and the ice age. Much of the rest of the story is modern history. The Earth's crust continues to move, even today, and with the shifts come earthquakes and volcanic eruptions. All things continue to change and move forward."

Thoth returned to the Great Room, carrying Crystal with him. He spoiled her so much.

"I heard that!" Thoth exclaimed, "She gives unconditional love and deserves to be properly cared for and loved in return."

I giggled.

"I've been reflecting on our trip and the greatness of the planet we live on," I said. "Nothing happens by accident. It is a massive and grand operation all designed and given life by the thought of our Creator, God, and it is perfection."

"Yes," mused Thoth. "This planet of ours goes through a delicate balancing act, not unlike thousands of other planets in the universe though. What makes this process unique is that this is our planet where we, humanity, lives.

"Unfortunately, for the past few centuries, humanity hasn't been a very good steward of our planet, the water, and the land masses. Recently, some people have placed a lot of emphasis on environmental issues, but those behind these movements have become divisive and corrupt. Yes, awareness of caring for the land, the plant life, trees, animals, oceans, and air are essential. But the planet has enough natural resources to overcome much of the damage of the last two centuries.

"What humanity must understand is that it needs to be stewards of the planet, not environmentalists. When trees are removed or harvested, people need to replace them. When land is overused by crop production, people need to let that land lay fallow for a year, rest, and grow a different crop there the following year, not add fertilizer. If there are too many cement cities, people need to create more parks. If forest land is too full with trees people need to thin the forest for safety from fire and disease and allow the other trees to mature into healthier trees.

"As to the climate, unless someone is deliberately choosing to scientifically manipulate the weather to bring harm to others, the climate runs in small to massive cycles. Climate changes are not the result of humanity's lifestyle but rather the life cycles of the planet itself and even the universe.

"Human life has cycles. People are born, grow up, mature, and then return back to the Creator. Likewise, planet Earth also has cycles of years where it is colder or warmer, rainier or dryer, has wind and rain storms or doesn't. Everyone and everything lives by cycles, including our magnificent planet Earth."

The Medicinal Chamber

I spent the next few days away doing human things in my above ground human life. When I arrived back at the outside entrance of the Library of Wisdom and Knowledge, the doors parted to let me pass through. I immediately saw Thoth standing on the other side. He walked over to greet me. Apparently, I arrived early as his intention was to meet me on the outside, not the inside.

We exchanged greetings and headed down the corridor to the Abode, talking through brain waves all the way, just catching up. It was good to be back. There was so much unconditional love energy in the space that it was hard to leave, and returning was always alluring, even seductive.

Thoth started right in, "Sit, eat, and drink. We have much to do. Would you like to go on another adventure? Everything is already prepared."

"Of course," I said. "I love the adventures you plan."

Within a few minutes we were back out in the corridor on a transport platform going up the long corridor we just walked down. We made a sharp right at the center cross. We traveled quite some distance down the second corridor before coming to a stop. We waited a moment for a typically large door on the right to open.

Thoth spoke, "Welcome to the Medicinal Chamber where we grow all our plants, herbs, flowers, and trees that provide us with all our healing supplies in addition to the crystals we use in the beds. Come, there is much to see."

It was a lovely area. The first room looked a bit like a futuristic domed glass house, greenhouse, or conservatory covering several acres. Far beyond its reach was an outdoor botanical garden. According to Thoth, there were many small walking paths that led to five smaller domed areas that had the necessary climate zoned features needed for the various plants in those areas. Little streams tumbled over rocks along the walkways and park benches were available to just sit and breathe in the healing fragrances, peace, and tranquility.

Thoth said, "This first area is filled with everything from roses to dandelions. The roses provide us rosehips we use for vitamin C. The rose petals are used for their oil and for healing scent, as well as to make rose water spray for purification. Dandelions are used for their beta carotene content and in the prevention or neutralization of free-radical type issues. In the distance you can see massive amounts of Queen Ann's Lace. Its root is a little like a carrot and can be eaten. You can dry the roots and use them as a warm beverage instead of coffee. They are also used as a poultice for wounds, ulcers, and sores. Turned into a tea like drink, it can be a diuretic and help release kidney stones.

"Off to the left are beds of lavender. Besides looking beautiful and smelling good, lavender is great for pain, bacterial infections, fungus issues, and even a sedative. Lavender scent on a pillow will help you relax and sleep better at night. The smaller rooms are devoted to what you would call traditional herbal plants. The Chinese have become the plant experts on herbal use as medicine. They have a well-care system for good health and use prevention instead of the disease care system most of the world uses."

We wandered for hours; one section was as amazing as the next. At first, I thought this to be a small area, but as we went through each of the smaller domed sections, I realized the area was at least a 200% increase of the original size I initially thought it was.

Thoth said, "We have now reached the botanical garden area with every tree and vine imaginable thriving somewhere within this beautiful area. Nut trees, seed trees and fruit trees are everywhere as long as they have some medicinal value.

"Come, let's eat and drink under one of your favorite trees," he said as he pointed the way to one of my all-time favorites, a fully blooming Royal Ponciana tree, sometimes called the Flame tree.

There it was in the center of the garden all dressed in its flaming orange glory. A magnificent tree that originated from Madagascar and Zambia, the Royal Ponciana tree has a breath-taking canopy of flowers. The color alone brings one joy. When the wind blows or the rain falls, the flowers drop to the ground and it looks like a flaming reddish orange velvet blanket.

Thoth interrupted my grand vision. "It is also medicinal. It can help with anything from menstrual cramps to inflammation and constipation. But for today, its purpose is to provide us with a beautiful place to rest and eat.

"This entire Chamber has only one purpose: to help people heal who are not well or to prevent health issues from occurring if someone is genetically pre-disposed.

"Far too little emphasis is being placed on prevention and natural medication in society today. Corporations would do a much better job of serving humanity and their investors if they sought out preventive measures, and insurance companies would do a much better job of serving their consumers by emphasizing a prevention and wellbeing care system versus a disease care system. Their financial rewards may go down a bit but the public support for them would dramatically rise.

"Come. Let's sit and enjoy the welcoming shade of one of your favorite trees. It's vibrant crimson-orange color nurtures the second or sacral chakra of the body, which nurtures creativity, sensuality, and intimacy. Creativity is at the forefront of your work right now so this is an important energy field for you."

Lifetimes of Connection and Gratitude

It was another beautiful morning in the Library of Wisdom and Knowledge. But then again, it was always another beautiful day in this peaceful place. Unconditional love, kindness, and nurturing oozed out of every corner, above, below, and within. It was a feeling hard to put into words as I had never experienced it before on Earth.

I sat on the sofa and watched the oversized candle flame glow from the equally oversized wick. I felt like I was in a meditative state as I gave expressions of gratitude for the magnificence of this space and for the presence of its master, Thoth.

Unknown to me, Thoth had entered the room and was observing my grateful heart.

He spoke, "You have always expressed gratitude for me, ever since we first met so many millennia ago. You were a beautiful child from a poor family and you were wearing ragged drab brown clothing, typical of that time period. I can still remember first meeting you when your mother took you to work with her one day at my aunt's house. You were quite the curious young lad, probably three or four years old at the time, and you asked me millions of questions.

"One day your mother asked me if I would take you as my student. By then you must have been six, maybe seven. Your new clothing was that of a long light-colored floor-length robe and a belt, much like the adults wore where I lived. You were so eager to learn and proud of your new life. When I lifted you up high in the sky you beamed with joy.

"You visited your mother often as your father was gone a lot, working on a sea faring cargo ship. You always ran back to my home with dozens of stories to tell. While our relationship was always teacher/student, we also became best of friends as you grew up.

"Then, one day, I ran to get you, grabbed you by the arm in a great hurry, placed you into a very strange air transport vessel you'd never seen before, and hid you so no one else could find you. At age 14 you understood the severity of our circumstances and silently hid as I went to get the others.

"Evil was trying to take control of Atlantis and unleash its power and control on the planet. Instead, Atlantis and the evil were destroyed by earthquakes from the deep and floods. Our home literally sank under the ocean as we took off. I know you couldn't see it from where you were hiding but you definitely felt it within.

"Finally, we landed in the new land of Khem, now known as Egypt, where the people were not yet educated. They were still ruled by physical force and lived in cave like dwellings. The people who came with us spread off into new areas of land to help educate the locals, create order out of chaos, and provide health guidance.

"It took me time to find a suitable home while you remained aboard the vessel with food and drink. Finally, I found a cave, which became the beginning of the Library of Wisdom and Knowledge. I returned to the ship to get you and we buried the ship in the earth in the dark of night for safe keeping, returning together to our new home. This is what that cave turned into after the passage of much time.

"You were just as grateful then as you are now so many millennia later. Your mother loved you so very much that she was willing to give you, her precious son, up so you could become something so much better than she could have offered."

By now tears streamed down my face. My gratitude was overflowing. I was gifted so much love by both my mother and Thoth so many ages ago. I felt overwhelmed.

Thoth continued, "Even though in those ages we were considered of different social status, we remained close. You were my scribe for many years. You watched my every move, recorded it for the Library, and remembered within all the truth, knowledge, and wisdom. But you never entered the Library out of respect for me. In fact, we sealed that wisdom and knowledge into your heart so that someday when we would meet again, we could unlock that information together for you to share with the world. You honored me and our Creator in all you did."

He took a couple of long deep breaths before continuing. "Many years later there were hostile uprisings around the country. One night you were heading home and were cornered by a small gathering of these aggressive hostile groups. They were seeking information from you about me, specifically how to bring me down and destroy our work and the Library. The more you refused to betray me, the angrier they got. They gave you one last opportunity to betray me. When you didn't, they killed you with a blow to the face.

"The next morning, when you weren't by my side at the usual time, I went looking for you. After I found your lifeless body, the locals told me what happened. Yes, we prosecuted the people who viciously took your life, but you were gone. My dearest friend was gone. I gave you a burial worthy of a pharaoh, but you were gone. A lifetime spent in each other's presence as companions, teacher/student, friends, brothers, was over except for the memories of that little boy who loved life so much. He would have followed me to the moon if that was our end destination."

Thoth stopped speaking when he realized that I was overwrought with emotion. He slowly stood up, came to me, and asked me to stand. I did. He then wrapped his strong arms around me, trying to console my sadness and grief. It felt like he had enormous ibis wings that enveloped me, allowing me to shed and let go of millennia's worth of grief, loss, disappointment, pain, and sadness.

Release of Grief and Renewing Energy

Yesterday was an emotional and difficult day. I never knew how Thoth and I parted ways in my lifetime as a scribe. The sadness came not from the way it ended, but from the disconnection from all the unconditional love Thoth gave me. He took me in, nurtured and nourished me, mentored me, and helped me grow into the honorable man I became. That was much to ask of another, especially a god of Atlantis. My heart ached for my deep loss then but also rejoiced for the gift of having him in my life today.

I sat at the table in the Great Hall with my two-flame candle burning. Thoth joined me and asked, "Are you better today?"

With a softened smile I said, "Yes. I am much better this morning. Thank you for telling me the story of how we began our first life together. Thank you, too, for the beautiful energy and love you gave me as you held me and wrapped me in your strength and unconditional love."

He replied, "You are very fortunate. Not many people have the opportunity or are ready to have past lives revealed, even though almost everyone has them. Not only was yours revealed right to your beginning, but you were also ready to receive the information and release all the grief and sadness you've experienced through the millennia. You don't need to re-visit each lifetime if you go directly back to the first experience, which is exactly what you did.

"You've carried on the giving of unconditional love by adopting (taking in) children of your own, and in turn your children adopting some your grandchildren. Unconditional love is in your heart, which is nurtured when you find a home like the Library of Wisdom and Knowledge. You are as much of a blessing here to us as we are to you."

We ate in silence and watched the candle flames flicker and dance as my mind reflected on everything from first meeting Thoth as a child to adopting my children to unconditional love.

Thoth finally broke the silence by saying, "I think we should go on an outing; your heart is still heavy and needs some joy."

As usual, he was right, so I nodded yes. Within minutes we were ready to go. A transport vehicle appeared in the corridor and whisked us away. Since the vehicle was not the type that could take us out into the universe, I knew our outing would be local.

"We are heading to one of my favorite places on planet Earth," said Thoth. "It is where I go when I want to be close to my Creator and be in total peace—something you could really use right now. We will be there soon."

As we descended to a lower altitude, I saw mountain tops jutting up through the clouds. As we got lower, I saw small green patches of grassy land. The mountain peaks were jagged, almost menacing from our up-close view, but they were covered with snow, which softened them a bit. As we continued to descend, I saw small patches of crisp, green, vegetation-covered land and cows grazing in some of the meadows below.

Thoth interrupted my thoughts and said, "Not only is that snow on the tops of the Alps, but under that snow are glaciers dating back to the Ice Age. With the glaciers are the melting ice flows that turn into rivers and thousands of waterfalls. I know you love and appreciate glaciers as much as I do. Their massive size, power, and ancient history is as enticing as is their beauty.

"There is a small meadow ahead that is impossible to reach by foot, making it secluded and private. We will land there and have a picnic. You will love this as much as I do, plus it should replenish some much-needed joy."

We stepped off our transport. I was expecting it to be icy cold but was pleasantly surprised at the warmth provided by the sun on this small protected meadow surrounded by nothing but glacier and snow-covered statuesque mountain tops. The only sounds were from the riverlets and waterfalls nearby. It was so pristine, crisp, and pure that only the Master's hand could have created this.

"The silence here is inviting, mesmerizing, even hypnotizing. I feel closer to our Creator here than anywhere else on planet Earth," said Thoth. "This is God's creation. The magnificence and majestic power of these peaks reach up to the heavens to honor the Creator and reflect the majesty, power, and strength of the Almighty. It is humbling yet inspiring at the same time. We may be at the mountain top but we are so humbly below the grandeur and greatness of our Creator."

As Thoth became silent, we ate and drank and basked in the sunlight and the nearness of our Creator's presence. Both of us fell into deep meditation until a crisp cold gust of wind swept through the meadow, indicating that the sun's warmth would be quickly swept away as it glided down behind the mountain tops.

"Come quickly," Thoth said. "It will be freezing cold in a matter of minutes. We must leave."

As quickly as we and our belongings got aboard, our transport rose straight up high above the Alps until we saw only the snow caps. Eventually, we traveled far enough that they disappeared into the distance.

Enroute back to the Abode, Thoth asked, "Are you feeling better? I see the glow of a bit of joy returning to your face." He turned to light the oversized candle with the very large wick.

Awareness

A few days later, Thoth and I sat at the table in peaceful quiet. I had just poured a nice hot cup of tea. Thoth said, "It is time to go. Are you ready?"

In my head I thought, "What? I just poured my tea." Out loud I said, "Where are we going? Must we leave right now?"

Thoth winked. "It's a secret. And yes, we must leave right now!"

I barely had time to finish my sip and off we went. We traveled on our floating platform at a speed I was not accustomed to. Thoth's face was aglow with excitement. He looked almost gleeful. However, once he finally looked at me and realized I was turning green from the speed, he slowed down a bit to a speed still fast but not a land version of warp speed.

"We're here," he announced as we stopped in the middle of nowhere. A new set of doors appeared and we passed through quietly into a totally dark space.

"We are in the Awareness Chamber where feelings are everything. No, not the touch with your hands type of feelings, but where your heart senses and feels everything. Where your awareness, perception, consciousness, and internal sensing are on high alert.

"In some ways, this is like your modern-day escape room where you need to figure out the clues on how to get out of the room. But in our chamber, you need to use your heart center, sensing and feeling to keep you on the right path."

Thoth must have felt some serious resistance on my part but continued, "There is nothing in here that can or will harm you, and nothing that will embarrass you or keep you from reaching the objective, which is unconditional love. And, the room is round so you cannot bump into corners and hurt yourself.

"After all, isn't that what you've already done in both of our lifetimes? You found your Creator within. It was a long and arduous journey but you never stopped seeking. It was scary at times. You spent many hours feeling lost and alone. But you continued your search until one day you found your answer, your direct connection to your Creator.

"This room represents that search, your search, everyone's search. There are five items in this room that provide you unconditional joy, your Creator connection, and love. You just need to use your heart center to find them in the dark. This is the path everyone uses in some form to find their Creator. I will be nearby should you need me."

My first inclination was to scream, LET ME OUT OF HERE, but I knew that was not the lesson Thoth wished for me to experience.

I thought for a bit. My first thought was that I should go to the right because most people walk along the right side and go right. But that would be the path most taken, and I should go on a path less taken.

I stepped forward a bit boldly as if holding a compass in my hand. I knew I was standing at due south. I decided to turn slightly left, southwest, and then proceeded. The closer I got to that area, the stronger I felt an energy field getting.

Then I found the source of the energy I felt. It was Crystal wagging her tail ever so happily but quietly so I could not hear her. For me, Crystal truly was the epitome of unconditional love and joy.

My next step was a slight right turn, maybe east or northeast. I proceeded slowly and cautiously but eventually I felt a welcoming energy field. I reached out and touched it. It was a lotus flower, the symbol of hope, regeneration, and going within. I painted this flower several times and it always gave me joy, but certainly not that deep unconditional joy and love I was seeking.

I was torn at this point. Should I turn left or right or go straight forward? I chose forward and moved across the room in sort of in a westerly direction. The distance seemed equally long but about half way across I noticed an energy tug to my left. I felt it when I crossed from Crystal to the lotus flower as well, but I moved on. Finally, I felt an energy field in front of me. It wasn't as warm and loving, but it was very strong, as if trying to pull me in. I felt for it. It was a book. I smiled, as the book represented wisdom and knowledge, which provides me an eternity of joy.

Where next, I wondered. I turned perhaps 40 degrees and headed toward what could be southeast. Again, as I passed near the center area of my journey, I felt a tug on the left side but stayed focused and continued forward to my next stop. I felt it internally. I sensed its vibration but struggled to discover what it was. Finally, I found a button and pushed it. Out came a beautiful and my favorite rendition of the Anniversary Song/Waltz composed by Josif Ivanovici in 1888 and made popular by Al Jolson in 1946. I loved this song; I had fond memories of being a young girl trying to take my first awkward dance steps with my father at an anniversary dinner party. I could listen to this song play for hours.

That was number four. Where was number five? I decided to turn, less than 40 degrees to the right, and headed what should have been north. I sensed an energy field in that area that felt welcoming. As I moved slowly in that direction, I felt the energy tug in the middle of the room on my left side again. Finally, I gave in and went toward the energy tugging at my heart. The closer I got, the stronger the unconditional love became. In fact, it became so overwhelming that tears started to form. But I couldn't find anything. It finally occurred to me to look up and reach up. There I found my silver thread of connection to my Creator, waiting for me right in the center of my heart where it has always been for millennia.

At that moment soft lights popped on as if my eternal connection lit up the room and my world.

Awareness Part Two

"You did well yesterday in the Awareness Chamber," reflected Thoth out loud.

I replied, "You were right. That is a good exercise for anyone to undertake when on a journey within."

"The first time one tries, they may only find one step or maybe two," Thoth explained. "That is okay because those first steps will lead to the next and the next. Also, that tells them exactly where they are on their spiritual journey.

"The more aware they become the more able they are to feel or sense their way to the next step. It is the draw of the unconditional love of our Creator that brings us complete joy. If that position is not reached by step five, their journey will simply be longer, needing more time and more steps.

"Sometimes they may find what they think is unconditional love or get confused with feeling joy along the way. For example, a child might receive a bike, or a young teen may get a mobile phone. While these gifts may provide instant joy, it is not unconditional love. Its influence or false joy is gone the moment they are bored with the materialistic item or misuse it.

"The same is true for adults, only they might find a boyfriend or girlfriend who is the ultimate joy, not recognizing that true joy and unconditional love comes from within, not another person. Again, like the bicycle or the phone, what happens when the relationship breaks up or is misused? Often, they seek yet another person to fulfill their joy. They keep repeating the cycle moving from one poor relationship to another, continually by-passing what already exists in the center of their heart.

"When you were in the darkness of the Awareness Chamber, you chose a longer path and three times passed by the greatest energy force in the universe, that of the unconditional love of the Creator. You felt it and noted it each time you passed until you could no longer ignore the deep energetic connection of your Creator within.

"You found some form of the unconditional love each place you stopped but you knew each time something was still missing. As you found the next step, the unconditional love moved you deeper within until you found yourself bathed in the unconditional love that is only available through our connection with our Creator, God, First Source, the ultimate giver of hope, peace, and joy."

The Next Chapter

The days passed and turned into weeks of one-on-one learning, wisdom, and knowledge firsthand through direct experience. Is it any wonder that I or anyone in my shoes would never want to leave this place of unconditional love, in-depth sharing of wisdom and knowledge, even love for my little dog Crystal? But as time passed here, the time to help and serve others in my human world drew closer.

"Nonsense," said Thoth, who was eavesdropping on my thoughts again. "Your time here in the Library with me, your equal colleague, never ends. You can join me at a moment's notice anytime from anywhere on the planet. You have unrestricted access to the Library, the Abode, and my time and information.

"Instead of dwelling on what lies ahead or fear of the future, take a deep breath and come back into the now, where we currently are, in this moment. We have work to do. Let's go."

I was surprised by Thoth's comments and forcefulness. I knew at that moment that no matter where life took me, Thoth would in some way be part of it, encouraging me, advising me, and teaching me. When you have a direct representative of the Creator as your personal guide, they are forever your guide.

I knew that during one's lifetime, a person can have many spiritual guides. Some arrive for a specific purpose and leave. Some are there only during youth. Others stay much longer or until the person needs different guides to fulfill their life purpose. Some are family members, like my grandmother, who come and go throughout life but are always nearby and on call.

And in my case, a guide comes when you are much further along in your spiritual journey. This guide stays with you for the rest of your life to help you fulfill your life purpose.

I was so grateful that Thoth boldly announced himself and pushed his way into my very being. It was a magnificent journey filled with joy, learning, experiencing, learning, time travel, testing, learning, tears, and joy. And oh, did I mention learning?

"Now who's the teacher?" interrupted Thoth. "Come. Let's leave, please."

As usual, Thoth was eager to teach and ready to go. Our hover transport awaited us in the corridor as we set off onto another adventure.

"We've arrived. Let's go," said Thoth as the door opened. "We are returning to the Galaxy Chamber; you need to see something very exciting in the stars. Let's sit and focus on the beautiful night sky.

"Look to the northern hemisphere and focus on the beautiful bird in the sky—one of the birds you've given your unconditional love to. Yes, there it is, the constellation Cygnus, the swan. Notice that a line from its tail star Deneb crosses through the big dipper and connects with the main star Regulus in Leo.

"If you were to continue that line from Regulus out into the universe and travel as far as we traveled to Galaxy 6, you would eventually reach the newest Galaxy, 7, brought to life by a single thought of our Creator. That is the magnificence of our Creator that creates the universe, the galaxies, and us, and is always connected to every human life on planet Earth."

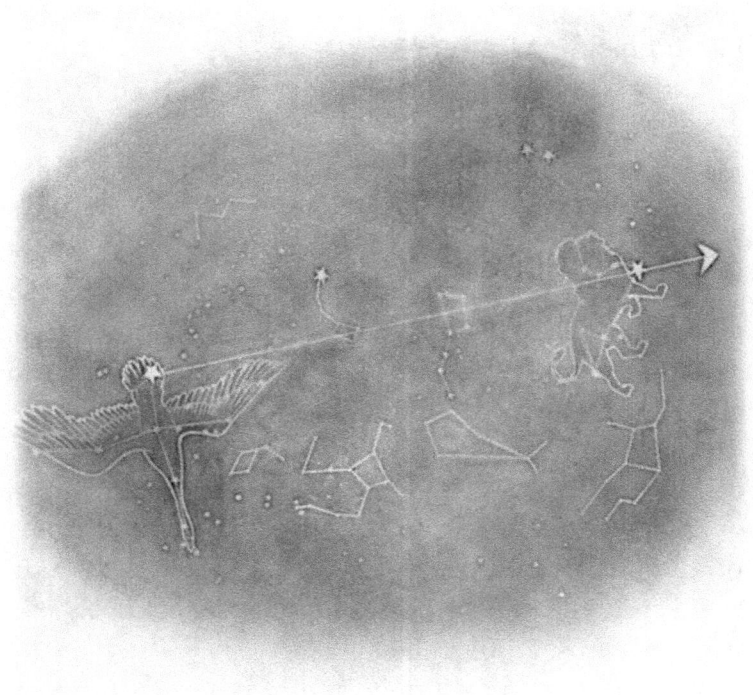

"It is truly the ultimate gift, the gift of life the Creator bestows upon us, not just the stars. It is humanity's responsibility as individuals to cherish and treasure that gift, take control of self, and accept full responsibility for nourishing and nurturing self to become the treasured human being that fulfills his or her life purpose in respect of self and of those they serve and in honor of their Creator."

Thoth paused for a moment and then continued.

"Enough thinking about endings and goodbyes. We will share time and space together wherever we are for eternity in the presence of our Creator.

"Let's go. Food and drink await us."

Epilogue

As Thoth spoke his last words ending the book, we rose from our seats, knowing that this was the end of our collaborative book journey. We embraced, holding onto what we have as a result of this collaboration, remembering fondly our past, and paying tribute not to the future but to our Creator that destined our lives to reunite after so many millennia.

Fully knowing this was only the beginning for us and what lies ahead, we both also felt a feeling of profound loss, knowing that a very good thing had come to an end.

"No more tears," said Thoth. "We have many years of working together ahead, which begins our new journey—one filled with hope, peace, and joy as you spread our Creator's message around the world."

The book may have ended but his words of working together for eternity kept ringing in my ears. I woke the next morning with Crystal by my side and reflected on all that had occurred since Thoth so boldly entered my world. My intent is that this collaboration changes the world for the better as much as it changed me and my life.

I feel so honored, so blessed, so much more in tune with Thoth and our Creator since experiencing such intense and meaningful experiences with them. I had a front row seat to the past and the future but did not realize that when I began journaling our collaboration. My gratitude for Thoth is sometimes so intense and overwhelming; he is so much bigger than life for me and hopefully for you the reader. In fact, I believe I've just scratched the surface on understanding his greatness, his depth, his knowledge and responsibilities in the universe, and his direct relationship with our Creator. It is both humbling and an honor.

I must admit that as a human, I was very afraid when the collaboration ended because I thought Thoth would be gone from my life. Gratefully, he is still here, waiting for me whenever I return to the Library of Wisdom and Knowledge. He always makes it very clear that I can return at any time whether he is there or not. It is actually very hard to not return there regularly because of all the unconditional love, peace, and joy that is ever present.

This book covers at least a half year or more of human time. The journaling took place every day, except for five days involving health issues, over a period of three plus months. The journaling sessions were very intense and never less than 90 minutes. Sometimes they ran 3 hours in length. Overall, the sessions averaged about two and a half hours per day. It was profound journaling, as it was delivered through a conversation, an experience, a connection, an adventure, and a teaching, as well as my commentary. While I can journal almost anywhere, I usually journal in my studio, which is dedicated to painting and writing. This type of journaling requires extraordinary attention to the flow of energy and information. Distractions can and do break that flow instantly. I usually use a simple spiral bound composition project planner book to write in. It allows me ample room to write but also to go back and make notes or corrections on the side panel.

Once I realized I was writing a book, not just having a personal conversation with Thoth, at least three weeks of entries passed filling numerous pages. That's when I started to enter each journaling session into my computer, which was the next step to turning my writing into a book. It took on average three to four hours per day to input the information, which always included some editing. The journaling and computer input took up to six or seven hours of my day. Some days I had to force myself to stop in order to prevent exhaustion. Only then was the final draft sent to my fabulous editor, who helped turn it into the book you are reading.

I eagerly looked forward to each and every morning to begin my journaling and my adventure for the day. In fact, I could hardly wait. In all my years of journaling, this is the first time I've experienced uncontrollable tears as I wrote. That happened twice during this journaling journey. During one session I was sobbing to the point that I had to stop and get control of myself before continuing, but then the tears would start all over again. I personally experienced very deeply every feeling, emotion, activity, and adventure as Thoth unveiled it to me. His words found their way deep into my heart and left me a better person, a more aware person, and a person on a much closer and deeper walk with my Creator.

While it is perhaps interesting to learn a little about how and where I write, I do hope you've been touched by Thoth's words. My wish is that his wisdom and knowledge will provide you a new roadmap to living a better life—one that puts you on a closer journey with our Creator.

If you think about it, I am still Thoth's scribe, a human, many millennia later, writing this book. And at this point I must admit that I do love when he addresses me as his Queen.

Thoth's Words of Wisdom

"Where there is truth and wisdom, love prospers."

*****

"Creativity is the key to opening the human's heart to its connection with the Creator. The First Source, the One, God was and is the master of creation. Without creation there would only be void. The easiest way for humanity to find their way back to their Creator is through creativity. Each person should dedicate a portion of their lives every week to creative activities. There are so many to choose from."

*****

"Creativity fills the heart with joy and reduces stress. It is an outlet that brings the human being back in control of their life and provides them peace within, allowing a spiritual flow of energy to freely move between the being and their Creator."

*****

"In order to create a reign of hope, peace, and joy, humanity needs to learn about astrology and its impact on societal behaviors. When they understand that, the leaders of a society can create a foundation that will maintain hope, peace, and joy during a 2,000-year passage of a difficult astrological house and then learn to blossom and create an even better society in the next more friendly age … The 21st century will be full of massive change for the better. It will give birth to a spiritual awakening, a revival and rebirth of the arts, music, literature, and wonderful advances in the areas of health care, not disease care, and technology."

*****

"Humankind is the Creator's most precious creation. Our Creator, God, First Source is part of each of us, just as much as we are each a part of the Creator. Like the individual raindrop becomes part of the mighty Nile, the mighty Nile is that drop of rain along with all the other previous drops of rain. You can't have one without the other. Collectively, we are humanity, but humanity is made up of diverse humans. Diversity is humanity."

*****

"Humanity does not yet understand the importance of each child. But their children are the future of the country and the planet. If they are not taught responsibility for others and the planet, and how to feed, nourish, and nurture each other, how will the planet survive?"

*****

"Manifest what you want. There is nothing standing in your way. Research no more. You know the way forward ... If it's a miracle you seek, manifest it. If it is volunteer help you need, manifest it. If it's a book on the New York Times bestsellers list, manifest it. Simply sit somewhere quiet, be in silence, and see clearly what you seek. If it is in alignment with who you are and what your life mission is, it will come to you. Nothing, not even yourself, can stand in your way."

*****

"Sound with string and wind instruments creates a healing experience for the human body, especially when you remove all other thoughts and distractions. When properly put together, music, nature, color, and fragrance are very healing for the body and mind."

*****

"For those who cannot silence their mind easily or at all, the flame of a candle or a fireplace relaxes you and opens your heart instead of your mind and ego. So many people think they must go through rituals to silence their mind, but all they really need is a burning candle flame or their hand. To use your hand, simply flatten your hand with the fingers together, and then place the clustered fingers flat on your third eye area just above and between your eyes. Then gracefully take the same flattened hand with connected fingers and lay it over your heart. It's important that every human knows how to silence their mind."

*****

"Your current world is very lopsided and will face total imbalance until they awaken enough to re-right the ship … Only societies based on equality, respect, and elf-control, the opposite energies from science and technology, can thrive. Only balanced life honoring the energies of the planet, meeting the needs of humanity, and living life in accordance with the intent of the Creator will thrive."

*****

"What gives you joy, so much that your heart overflows? What provides you the most relaxation, refueling, and restoration? You need to know this to manifest it. All humans need to know this so they can continually refuel and restore self for peak performance."

*****

"Humans need acknowledgement and to feel appreciated. Those two things lead the way to respect and equality. When you acknowledge and appreciate the small things, the large things become much easier. You cannot constantly berate humans or animals and expect them to perform their best. But when you nurture and nourish them with kindness and appreciation, they will blossom and produce. Even the beautiful blue lotus flower finds nourishment in the muck of the Nile and blossoms."

*****

"All of the scientists in the world sought the magic of the philosopher's stone, thinking it would turn something into gold. The thing that each of them missed was that they all had the philosopher's stone within. All they had to do was go within and reconnect with their Creator. The real philosopher's stone was the unconditional and infinite love they would find when connected to their eternal One Source, God, the Creator, not fool's gold that can be lost, given away, or stolen at a moment's notice."

*****

"Humanity does not understand the impact of words used by others. Nor do they understand the full impact of words they say to themselves within their own minds. Just as societies can be driven into war with the use of specific words, so can a person drive themselves into defeat before they even begin."

*****

"Words matter. Words create everything in your life and in the universe. Use words that are encouraging, uplifting, and empowering at all times. You can't create something good, powerful, uplifting, and joyful from negative words and thoughts. You can't create or manifest a better life if you are focused on the negative. No matter how hard you try, you cannot attract something good from something bad."

*****

"If your thoughts are in your highest and best interest and bring no harm to others, then you are on the right path. If you are constantly putting yourself and others down, stop and think about how you are destroying yourself and perhaps others as well."

*****

"Humans are so busy doing the unimportant that they forget the important. They forget to care for those they love, including themselves, and to find their joy in life. Joy can be found in the smallest rose bush to the largest piece of quarried marble, from a beautifully polished piece of lapis jewelry to a puppy eagerly wagging its tail. Humans have given up these moments of joy in return for spending endless hours of time on their electronic gadgets and big screen televisions instead of sharing their time with loved ones, friends, and neighbors. Perhaps even more important, they block the connection they have with their Creator, the ultimate giver of joy."

*****

"The more you can show and express your gratitude for all things, large or small, the faster the world will heal and the quicker humanity will be able to live in peace and harmony. People need to respect and honor equality in others and maintain self-control before they will find peace. Societies as a whole need to respect and honor other societies before peace can reign in a nation. And nations need to do the same before peace can engulf the world. And it all begins with the smallest of kind gestures and acts of appreciation."

*****

"Every human is born with a purpose. Most ignore it, might not know it even exists, or put it off until late in life when they are no longer able to complete their purpose. They don't realize how important they are to their Creator—the One who is in constant contact with them … Every person is a much-loved child of the Creator God and is given a special job to perform while on Earth. Every task is equally important; one is not better or more important that the other. Only the human mind and others trying to control you for their gain could be that divisive, trying to undermine your greatness."

*****

"The human was never designed by the Creator to deal with the volume of stress that attacks it daily ... In the 21st century, it has reached the tipping point for humanity. Every stressor from early millennia is still affecting humanity, with greed and control heaped on top. The level of stress has exponentially increased with the addition of mega political factions trying to take over the world and the incessant intrusion of technology. Humanity has no escape route unless they adopt a lifestyle that includes stress relaxing measures. Parks should have labyrinths, even if it is only a footpath marked by stones. Corporations should build stress relieving labyrinths within their walls and in outdoor spaces where weather permits. Large family neighborhoods should include labyrinths in the original plan of the development. If these kinds of steps are not taken, natural immunity levels will continue to decline and humanity will morph into a disease-prone, Godless, chaos-filled abyss. Humanity must act now and reverse this massive invisible trend."

*****

"If you want to see your Creator, look into the eyes of a newborn child; the Creator resides there. That physical birth is proof of the Creator's existence."

*****

"Humanity continues to look without when they need to look within. The answers to the future greatness of humankind all lie within. They cannot achieve the abundant love and joy the Creator has stockpiled for each and every child of the universe without looking within and seeking transformation."

About the Author

Pat Heydlauff is an expert at designing home and workplace environments that reduce stress, improve work/life balance, increase prosperity, and build knowledge in Feng Shui principles. She provides people with a roadmap that's crucial for navigating through today's chaos, technological interruptions, and financial dictates. Through the 7 Divine Principles from *Looking Within*, she helps people open their hearts so they can see the truth, open their ears to hear the Divine's whispers, and open their thinking so they can love, flourish, and connect.

Known as "The Renaissance Woman" Pat is a Flow of Focus Strategist; Work/Life Balance, Prosperity, and WorkForce Expert; and Feng Shui Expert. She is certified in Organization Management, Neuro Linguistic Programming, and Time Line Therapy. She is also the founder of the groundbreaking "Flow of Focus" System for Leadership & Efficiency.

Pat's mission is to help individuals unlock their full potential to live a truly stress-free, prosperous, and meaningful life, and to guide businesses to a path of maximum productivity, profitability, and efficiency.

Contact her at www.PatHeydlauff.com.

www.ingramcontent.com/pod-product-compliance
Lightning Source LLC
Chambersburg PA
CBHW070758020526
44118CB00036B/1906